INDIVIDUAL FOCUS

AF761792

# Class Interrupted

## Strategies for Positive Behaviour

PEARSON

Copyright ©2008, the Crown in Right of Alberta, as represented by the Minister of Education. Alberta Education, Learning and Teaching Resources Branch, 10044–108 Street NW, Edmonton, Alberta, Canada, T5J 5E6

All rights reserved. This publication is protected by copyright and permission should be obtained from the publisher prior to any prohibited reproduction, storage in a retrieval system, or transmission in any form or by any means, electronic, mechanical, photocopying, recording, or likewise. For information regarding permission, write to the Permissions Department.

ISBN-13: 978-0-13-704003-2
ISBN-10: 0-13-704003-2

Vice-President, Publishing: Mark Cobham
Vice-President, Marketing and Professional Field Services: Anne-Marie Scullion
Research and Communications Manager: Chris Allen
Managing Editor: Joanne Close
Project Editor: Elizabeth Salomons
Senior Production Editor: Lisa Dimson
Proofreader: Kate Revington
Production Coordinator: Zane Kaneps
Interior Design and Composition: David Cheung
Permissions Coordinator: Jamie Whittla
Cover Design: David Cheung
Cover Image Credit: Spohn Matthieu/PhotoAlto Agency RF Collections/Getty Images

For permission to reproduce copyrighted material, the publisher gratefully acknowledges the copyright holders.
2 3 4 5 6 WC 17 16 15 14 13

Printed and bound in Canada.

PEARSON

# Table of Contents

# Acknowledgments


## Senior Advisors

Dr. Avis Glaze
Founding CEO, Literacy and Numeracy Secretariat, and Former Ontario Education Commissioner and Senior Advisor to the Minister of Education, Ontario

Ruth Mattingley
Former Superintendent of Education, Lambton Kent District School Board, and Former Senior Executive Officer, Literacy and Numeracy Secretariat, Ministry of Education, Ontario

## Teacher Advisor

Jan Kielven
Former Student Achievement Officer, Character Development, Literacy and Numeracy Secretariat, Ministry of Education, Ontario; currently, Positive Climates for Learning Specialist, Curriculum and Instruction, York Region District School Board

## Reviewers

Linda Galen
Coordinating Principal, Secondary Curriculum and Instruction Support, Peel District School Board

Kim Gleim
Acting Co-ordinator, Student Behaviour Supports, Saskatoon Public Schools

Kim Hutchinson
Teacher, Ottawa Catholic School Board

Yrsa Jensen
Director of Programs, BC Educational Leadership Council

Jeanette Johnston
Learning Supervisor, Special Education, Thames Valley District School Board

Dianne Kay
Learning Specialist, Student Services, School District 18, New Brunswick

Lynn Landry
Literacy Leader, Halifax Regional School Board

Laura McCarthy
Coordinator, Academic Staff Development, Dufferin-Peel Catholic District School Board

Lisa Millar
Superintendent of Education, Pickering Schools, Durham District School Board

Barb Nathoo
Principal, London District Catholic School Board

Carmen Oliveira
Teacher, Toronto District School Board

Joyleen Orescanin
Special Education Consultant, Prairie South School Division

Bernie Ottenheimer
Psychologist, Safe and Caring Schools Consultant, Department of Education, Government of Newfoundland and Labrador

Donna Rice
Principal, Toronto District School Board

Craig Runciman
Principal, Rainbow District School Board

Kim Sullivan
Coordinator of Assessment, Evaluation, and Reporting, Chignecto-Central Regional School Board

Pauline Thornton
Integrated Services Coordinator, Trillium Lakelands District School Board

Karen Topper
Literacy Improvement Project Teacher, Hamilton-Wentworth District School Board

Mike Walter
Superintendent, Instruction and School Services, Regina Public Schools

## Original Edition Team (Supporting Positive Behaviour)

**Principal Writer**
Dwaine Souveny

**Contributing Writers**
Dana Antayá-Moore
Karen Bain
Darci Fulton
Brenda Sautner

# Foreword

Schools by their very nature provide a setting in which to nurture the attributes of a civil society. Integral to this concern is the need for schools to prepare students for citizenship in its broadest form. It is essential that we provide students with an education that enables them to think critically, feel deeply, and act wisely.

For communities and countries to meet the challenges of the 21st century, our schools will have to establish high expectations for students and utilize the strategies identified by the effective schools research. One key characteristic of effective schools is a safe and orderly environment. Research has clearly shown that when students feel safe and are able to learn in an environment that supports positive behaviour, their achievement improves.

Respect and empathy form the basis for positive interpersonal relationships. When students, regardless of their background or circumstances, learn to respect one another, it provides a positive learning culture. In this context, students come to value the rights and opinions of others and learn how to resolve issues positively and collaboratively. Of equal importance is the quality of empathy, which is the essence for human caring and concern. When students can empathize across the lines that divide us in society, they are more likely to demonstrate caring and concern within the broader community. This results in sowing the seeds of social cohesion in our schools, which, in turn, benefits the larger society.

The world that our students will inherit is becoming more complex and demanding. Our students will be living in a more diverse society, which means that they must learn to respect diversity in all of its forms within that society. Leading futurists tell us that minorities will become majorities, and for the first time in history, the old will outnumber the young. All of these societal changes will require that we inculcate in students the skills, attitudes, dispositions, and positive behaviours necessary for our society to thrive.

School districts across Canada and beyond have identified the development of a safe and orderly school environment as a top priority, one essential to student success and school improvement. When negative behaviour issues are prevalent, learning, instruction, and school climate are compromised. Creating a learning environment that facilitates positive behaviour requires a whole-school effort.

Schools cannot achieve a safe environment alone, however. Communities and schools need to collaborate fully to build the alliances and coalitions necessary to ensure positive behaviour. Educators must work together to implement effective strategies that will result in productive learning environments for all students. To achieve this goal, school administrators and teachers will require effective strategies, such as those provided in this three-part resource.

***Class Interrupted: Strategies for Positive Behaviour*** provides information, strategies, stories from schools about what works, and sample tools for systematically teaching, supporting, and reinforcing positive behaviour. This integrated system of school-wide, classroom, and individual supports is designed to provide school staff with effective strategies to improve behaviour in their schools. The goal of this approach is to facilitate both students' academic achievement and healthy social development in a safe, supportive learning environment.

Creating positive learning environments requires a team approach. Everyone shares in the responsibility for shaping a safe and orderly school climate. In some circumstances, though, even with the best of intentions, educators do not have the resources to achieve this goal. ***Class Interrupted: Strategies for Positive Behaviour*** provides effective strategies that have been informed by research and shown to work in a variety of settings. It is a flexible approach that recognizes the diversity within each school.

Both elementary and high school educators will benefit from use of this resource. Every attempt has been made to provide age appropriate examples. We are confident that both new and experienced teachers and administrators will find many insights, examples, and strategies that will enhance their ability to support positive behaviour in their schools and classrooms. They will be able to act in a proactive and intentional manner.

Public schools are the foundation of our democracy. Our schools today have the potential not only to reflect, but to shape and create anew the society that we all cherish. Canada is an example for the world because of our commitment to achieve excellence, equity, and empathy for others. When educators ensure that human relations, as well as interpersonal and behavioural issues, are addressed appropriately, our students will soar to new heights of performance and attainment. ***Class Interrupted: Strategies for Positive Behaviour*** provides the tools to achieve this vision.

Dr. Avis Glaze
Ruth Mattingley

# Introduction

Drawing on current research and best practices, this third part of the three-part resource, *Class Interrupted: Strategies for Positive Behaviour*, presents information and strategies for providing intensive, individualized support and instruction for the small percentage of students requiring this level of intervention.

This system of individual student support is designed to provide teachers with effective strategies to improve behavioural outcomes for students with behaviour disabilities. The goal of this approach is to facilitate academic achievement and healthy social development of students in a safe, supportive classroom environment.

The following pyramid model illustrates the behavioural issues in a typical student population. Studies (Martella and Nelson, 2003; Gresham, 2004) show that 80 to 85 percent of students generally meet the school's behavioural expectations. Another 5 to 15 chronically do not meet expectations and are at risk of developing severe behaviour disabilities. One to 7 percent have behaviour difficulties severe enough that they cannot meet behavioural expectations without intensive, individualized interventions.

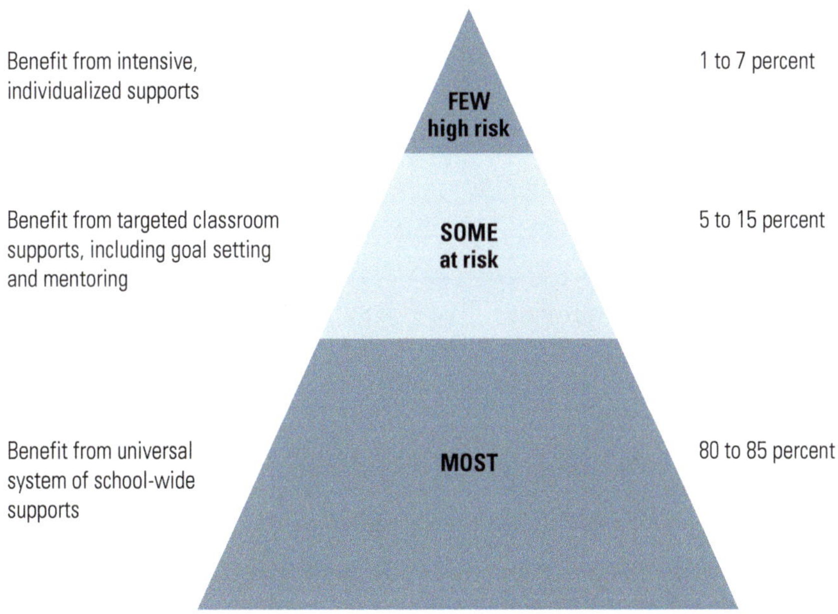


**Three-tiered model of positive behaviour support**

The three tiers of this model represent a continuum of increasingly intense interventions that correspond to the responsiveness of students.

- All students will benefit from a **universal system of supports**, and for 80 to 85 percent, this is sufficient to maintain positive behaviour.

- More **targeted interventions**, such as social skills instruction and behavioural management, will benefit the 5 to 15 percent of students who are at risk of developing serious behaviour problems even when universal supports are provided.
- **Intensive, individualized supports** will benefit the 1 to 7 percent of students who do not respond to universal and/or targeted interventions.

This three-part resource, *Class Interrupted: Strategies for Positive Behaviour,* is organized around this model. The three books deal with

- a **universal** school-wide approach
- a **targeted** classroom management approach
- an **intensive**, individualized approach

This resource, *Class Interrupted: Strategies for Positive Behaviour (Individual Focus),* focuses on the top part of the pyramid—those students with behaviour disabilities. School staff may also wish to refer to the other two parts of the resource to create a comprehensive approach to positive behaviour.

Students with behaviour disabilities generally benefit from effective classroom management and a school-wide approach that supports positive behaviour, but their individual needs go further. These students require intensive, individualized supports to prevent problem behaviour, teach new social competencies, and respond to aggressive behaviour.

## Characteristics of Students with Behaviour Disabilities

Students with behaviour disabilities exhibit chronic and pervasive behaviours that are so maladaptive that they interfere not only with the individual student's learning and safety but also with the learning and safety of other students. Students with behaviour disabilities typically demonstrate several observable maladaptive behaviours, including

- an inability to maintain satisfactory relationships with peers or adults
- inappropriate behaviours or feelings under ordinary conditions
- difficulty accepting appropriate levels of personal responsibility and accountability
- threatening and/or physical aggression toward other people and/or physical destruction of the environment

For resources about educational programming for student with behaviour disabilities, see our Web site: www.pearsoncanada.ca/ci

# Understanding Key Elements

There are 10 key elements of support for students with behaviour disabilities. These elements are interrelated and may have differing degrees of importance, depending on the needs, strengths, and priorities for a particular student.

1. **Positive relationships** between teachers and students, individual students and their peers, and teachers and parents
2. **Modification of the classroom environment** that ensures that the physical environment and routines support positive behaviour and reduce opportunities for problem behaviour
3. **Differentiated instruction** that looks for ways to restructure learning tasks and activities, considers the timing of activities, and teaches strategies for academic success
4. **Understanding individual student behaviour**, including the goals or functions of behaviour, and the escalation cycle
5. **Social skills instruction** that provides structured and intensive interventions to help students learn new behaviours that replace problem behaviours
6. **Positive reinforcement** that motivates students to use new social skills and demonstrate positive behaviour consistently and independently
7. **Fair and predictable consequences** for behaviour that adversely affects the student, other students, and/or the school community
8. **Collaborative teamwork and a wraparound process** that support the individual student, the classroom teacher, other school staff, and the student's family
9. **Data-informed decision-making** that clearly identifies and describes behaviours that need improvement and measures progress over time
10. **Individual behaviour support plans** that describe the specific steps the school team will take to change problem behaviour and maintain safety in the classroom

# 1 Positive Relationships

> "We encourage you to have clear, consistent rules and parameters and fair, meaningful consequences. But above all, be strong role models for your students and form positive, caring relationships."
>
> – Mark Boynton and Christine Boynton, *The Educator's Guide to Preventing and Solving Discipline Problems*

The development of positive, caring relationships is important for all students and is crucial for students with behaviour disabilities. These students often feel isolated and disconnected from others, both at home and at school. They will need many opportunities and intensive support and coaching in order to develop the social skills needed for successful relationships with both peers and adults.

## Teacher–Student Relationships

Having at least one significant relationship with a positive role model can make a significant difference in the life of any student, but this is especially true for the student who has a behaviour disability. A positive relationship with the teacher can also be a model for other students and can help foster a student's sense of belonging to the school community.

### Sample Strategies for Developing Positive Teacher–Student Relationships

- *Be positive.*
  Intentionally give individual students positive feedback at least four times for every one time you give corrective feedback.
- *Identify each student's genuine strengths and interests.*
  Make it your goal to identify at least five positive qualities or characteristics for any student with behaviour disabilities in your classroom; for example, reads well, helps younger students, has a sense of humour, has musical skills, and is a leader. Then let the student know that you recognize these qualities. One way of doing this could be to identify a different quality with the student each Monday and then look for opportunities throughout the week to highlight and reinforce behaviours that demonstrate this quality.

- *Tell other adults and students in the school about individual students' positive qualities.*
  Too often, staff hear only the problem behaviours of students who have behaviour disabilities. Look for opportunities to share good news about these students.

- *Create opportunities for students to be helpers and leaders in the classroom and school.*
  Look for ways to capitalize on one or more of their individual strengths or interests.

- *Refrain from criticizing students in front of their classmates.*
  Even though you avoid using labels, the student and others in the room who hear the criticism may internalize an implicit label. For example, if a teacher says publicly, "Keep your focus; you're tuning out," the student and peers may begin to believe the student is incapable of paying attention or may label himself or herself as having an attention problem.

## Use Hopeful and Respectful Language

Words are powerful tools for shaping ideas, perceptions, and attitudes. Because the kinds of words you use are so important, ensure your choice of language is positive and professional when talking *with* and *about* students with behaviour disabilities.

Choosing your words thoughtfully when sharing information about these students can be instrumental in overcoming negative attitudes and in shaping more positive ones. Hopeful and respectful language also demonstrates a sensitivity and awareness of the feelings and comfort level of these students and their families.

- *People first, then the behaviour or the disability.*
  Use terms such as "a student who has behaviour disabilities" rather than a "behaviour-disordered student." It is never acceptable to refer to an individual student or group of students as "the behaviour disordered" or by their special education designation.

- *Acknowledge the diversity of students who have behaviour disabilities.*
  There is a wide range of variance in the characteristics, strengths, needs, and life circumstances of students with behaviour disabilities. Avoid language that encourages stereotypes such as "*All* students with behaviour disabilities ..."

- *Be objective and nonjudgmental.*
  When talking about students with behaviour disabilities, choose words that are nonjudgmental and nonemotional, and are accurate descriptions. Focus on facts rather than perceptions. Avoid words and images designed to evoke pity or guilt such as "impaired by" or "handicapped."

## Look After Yourself[1]

Working with students with behaviour disabilities can be emotionally demanding of school staff. Self-awareness is a key component for managing stress. By taking proactive steps to increase their own self-awareness, staff who work with students with behaviour disabilities can

- build more positive relations with students
- minimize power struggles
- enhance their effectiveness

Increased self-awareness involves a more accurate understanding of how students affect our own emotional processes and behaviours, and how we affect students, as well. Our development as teachers depends on our willingness to take risks and regularly ask ourselves which of our own behaviours are helping or hindering our professional growth.

### Recognize Your Own Triggers

Although school staff need to learn how to recognize signs of emotional stress in their students, it is equally important to acknowledge that staff's own personalities and experiences have helped shape their attitudes and responses to certain behaviours.

Working with students who are in emotional turmoil can be stressful. Consistently responding in a calm and professional manner takes conscious effort. School staff who are aware of their own emotional triggers are more likely to minimize the frequency and intensity of counterproductive power struggles.

### Use Positive Reinforcement

Most school staff recognize the power and necessity of using positive reinforcement. By consciously noticing and reinforcing positive behaviour, the classroom becomes a more positive environment. However, teachers who work with students with behaviour disabilities can become so attuned to problem behaviours, they inadvertently neglect to recognize and build on positive behaviours and strengths. Systematically self-monitoring your own use of praise will increase the likelihood that you will use praise and encouragement more consistently and frequently. A number of research studies show that when the rate of positive reinforcement increases, the classroom becomes a happier and less stressful place for both students and staff.

1. From "The Importance of Teacher Self-Awareness in Working with Students with Emotional and Behavioral Disorders" by Brent G. Richardson and Margery J. Shupe, *Teaching Exceptional Children*, Volume 36, No. 2, 2003, pp. 8–12. Copyright 2003 by The Council for Exceptional Children. Reprinted with permission.

**The Penny Transfer Technique**

This is a simple strategy for shifting your focus from problem behaviour to positive behaviour.

1. Take five pennies and place them in your left pocket.
2. Identify students who regularly need prompting and reminders. Choose an individual student whose behaviour is interfering with learning.
3. Every time you are able to verbally encourage that student for something he or she does well, transfer a penny to your right pocket. Your goal is to move all five pennies to the right pocket by the end of the day.
4. Repeat this exercise each day for two weeks.
5. After one week, take a few minutes to reflect on how this strategy has affected your behaviour.
   - Are you beginning to automatically notice positive behaviours of more students?
   - Has this changed the behaviour of the student? What kind of data do you need to collect to answer this question?

## Talk with Colleagues

School staff need safe places to express their feelings and frustrations, and recharge their emotional batteries. Talking with supportive colleagues and community partners who work in the school is one of the most effective coping strategies. At all times, the confidentiality of the student and the situation must be respected.

## Use Humour

Many educators feel that an appropriate sense of humour is absolutely essential for long-term success in working with students. Students with behaviour disabilities often are trying to make sense out of a variety of highly charged emotional stressors (e.g., changing family structure, neglect and abuse, limited reading skills) and some students may direct their hurt and frustration at school staff and peers.

A study (Talbot and Lumden, 2000) found that teachers who were more likely to use humour in their classroom reported lower emotional exhaustion and a higher sense of personal accomplishment. An appropriate sense of humour is also an effective strategy for engaging students who seem to be disengaged. Humour can be one of the most effective means of de-escalating potential crisis situations.

Humour that heals (rather than hurts)

- is sensitive
- is good natured
- defuses difficult situations
- brings people closer together

Having a sense of humour in the classroom is less about telling jokes and more about maintaining a relaxed and upbeat attitude and outlook about work and life's twists. School staff who have an appropriate sense of humour convey to students that they enjoy their work and enjoy their students.

### Acknowledge Ways You Make a Difference in Students' Lives

School staff who perceive themselves as having the ability to bring about positive change to student behaviour and learning are more likely to perceive students as teachable and worthy of attention and effort. These school staff are also less likely to personalize the problem behaviour of students and more likely to maintain an empathetic attitude toward students who are challenging. Recognizing ways that they and others make a difference can affect the school staff's belief and commitment that they have the capacity to positively affect student performance and well-being.

## Build Home–School Partnerships

Students with behaviour disabilities particularly benefit from a strong collaboration between professional supports, school staff, and families. Teachers will often need to build rapport and a trusting relationship with parents in order to have effective discussions regarding behaviour programming, consequences, and interventions. Many families with students who have behaviour disabilities have negative and unresolved conflicts related to past experiences with school and are not always open to involvement.

Some parents of students with behaviour disabilities may not be comfortable attending formal school meetings, particularly if they haven't attended such meetings before. In challenging or difficult situations, parents' care and concern for their child might show up as tension, anxiety, or frustration. Teachers must remain nonjudgmental and avoid making assumptions. The parents' behaviours do not necessarily reflect how they truly feel or how they are actually coping. Emotional and other issues may get in the way of promoting an atmosphere of collaboration.

Following are some examples of parental and family issues the school may have to deal with.

- Parents who struggled at school themselves may be intimidated and feel uncomfortable about working in partnership with teachers.
- Parents may feel guilty or think they are in some way responsible for their child's difficulties. Some families may struggle with feelings of loss, grief, or embarrassment as they try to come to terms with their child's behaviour disabilities.
- Family situations can make participating in the child's education a challenge; for example, parental conflict, shift work, language barriers, or having more than one child with behaviour disabilities.
- The parents' culture may include a belief that school and home are separate.
- Parents may have issues of trust and need time to become comfortable talking about their child.
- Parents may not have confidence in the school's ability to provide adequate support for a student with behaviour disabilities.
- Some parents find it difficult to believe that their child has different needs than other children, particularly if their child does not experience the same degree of difficulty outside of the school environment or if the child shares behavioural characteristics of other family members.
- Parents and school staff may have differing opinions about a child's particular diagnosis, what that means in terms of expectations and how severe the current problem behaviour is.

Involving parents requires time, trust, and a belief that parents are partners in their child's education. Teachers can take a guiding role, particularly in the early stages, to help parents become actively engaged and committed to the process. Teachers need to help parents understand the value of a team approach to planning for behaviour support and the role they, as parents, can play in ensuring that the support accurately reflects their child's strengths and areas of need.

Take time at the outset to provide information and discuss what both parents and school staff hope to get out of these meetings. Doing this will help foster an atmosphere of openness and partnership with parents. As parents become more comfortable with their child's school team, they will more readily share information and perspectives that affect their child's learning.

## Sample Strategies for Encouraging Parental Participation

- *Maintain an open door policy.*
  Let parents know that they are welcome to visit the classroom to observe and participate in their child's learning. Provide information about how to do this during the first open house of the school year or through the classroom newsletter. Encourage parents to share their expertise and participate in special events, field trips and presentations, and other learning activities.

- *Acknowledge the parents' role and their contribution to their child's school team.*
  Parents need to know that school staff value their expertise and input. Children can act differently in various settings so to truly understand a child's behaviour, it is essential to include parents' perspectives and experiences.

- *Be prepared to answer parents' questions.*
  For example, parents might ask about the individual behaviour support plan for their child.
  - How will we be involved?
  - Do we attend all planning meetings for our child? If not, how do we keep informed about information shared and decisions made at those meetings?
  - When are the meetings held, and how long are they?
  - How can our child be a part of this process?
  - What kind of special support will my child receive?
  - Will my child always need this kind of support?
  - How is the individual behaviour support plan this year different from the plan for other school years? Can we change it at any time during the school year?
  - How will we know if the plan is effective?
  - How can we arrange to visit the classroom to see how our child is doing?
  - What are we expected to do at home to support our child?
  - What are our family's responsibilities regarding homework?
  - How are we expected to reinforce positive school behaviour at home?
  - How can we communicate with teachers?
  - What does our signature mean on the individual behaviour support plan and the individualized education or program plan? What happens if we don't sign them?
  - What are our options if we don't agree with the plans?

– How will progress be reported?

– Will my child always be on an individual behaviour support plan?

- *Use parent–teacher meetings as opportunities to develop partnerships.* Make meetings personal and positive. When possible, offer parents a choice of meeting times and communicate directly with them through a written notice or phone call. Give them sufficient time to arrange their schedule. Make sure the meeting notice gets to parents. Since students may neglect to pass a message along, a follow-up phone call may be necessary. Always provide information about how to contact the school in case parents have to reschedule a meeting. If possible, share an agenda of the meeting ahead of time so parents have a chance to think about the kinds of questions they want to ask and the issues they would like to discuss.

- *Make effective use of behaviour support plan meetings.* Allow time for questions and discussion. Share information about the child's behavioural needs. The more knowledgeable parents are about their child's behaviour and learning challenges, the better partners they can be. Resources might include copies of relevant articles and the addresses of new Web sites, and information about upcoming conferences or relevant parent workshops. Have someone keep a record of the action items and provide a copy to all team members.

- *Ensure that parents understand the kinds of decisions that need to be made when developing a behaviour support plan and then ask them to think about which aspects of the plan they would like to have input into.* For example, parents may wish to share their child's strengths, areas of need, information about how he or she learns best, medical information, successful strategies used at home, and goals they would like to see addressed in the plan. Encourage parents to speak with their child about his or her strengths, areas of need, and potential goals, and to share this information as well.

TOOL

Tool 1 provides tips for parents who are participating in the behaviour support planning process.

## Sample Strategies for Increasing Parents' Participation and Comfort Levels at Meetings

- *Consider convenience and comfort.* Arrange meetings at mutually convenient times and in a comfortable and appropriate place.

- *Be sensitive about the parents' comfort level.* Take this into consideration when determining how many school staff members will attend the meetings.

- *Provide parents with information about the purpose of the meeting and what will be discussed ahead of time.* This gives parents time to think about the items to discuss and to collect relevant information to bring to the meeting.

- *Think about the valuable information parents might have to share.* Include a list of questions with the meeting notice or proposed agenda. For example:
  - Are there changes at home that may be affecting your child's behaviour, such as a new family member, a change in a parent's work schedule, or new after-school activities or daycare arrangements?
  - Are there new supports for the child, such as time spent with a mentor or older student?
  - Have there been recent medical or other types of assessments or treatments?
- Encourage parents to make a list of key questions they want discussed during the first and subsequent meetings.
- Use the arrangement of chairs and tables to establish an atmosphere of collaboration and equity to encourage discussion.
- *Consider using chart paper and markers to record actions that are agreed on during the meeting.* This technique makes the process more visible for all participants.
- *Value the information that parents provide.* Schedule time during meetings for reflection and discussion.

## Resolving Differences

There are a number of strategies for resolving differences that may arise between parents and school staff. The first course of action is to try to resolve issues directly with the people who are working with the student. This means meeting as a school team and looking for positive ways to reach agreements that everyone is satisfied with.

### Tips for Handling Conflict and Resolving Differences with Parents

- Establish that the child's interests must come first at all times.
- Make it clear that you want to resolve the differences for future mutual benefit (e.g., "I appreciate your willingness to ..." or "I'm committed to finding a plan that will work for everyone").
- Deal specifically with solutions to the identified issues and be prepared to offer alternatives.
- Focus on the issues, not the emotions and the personalities of participants or events from the past that are no longer relevant.

- Ask parents to state their understanding of the situation and then paraphrase what you have heard.
- Separate the behaviours from the student and use neutral nonjudgmental language.
- Strive to accurately understand the parents' concerns and perspectives. Sometimes a disagreement occurs as a direct result of a misunderstanding.
- Always clarify exactly what the issue is from all perspectives before jumping ahead to solutions.
- Decide what you can compromise on. Effective resolution often requires some form of compromise, especially when issues are emotional and complex.
- Be sure that expectations for the student and the programming supports are realistic and reasonable.
- Explicitly state that you are committed to the agreed-upon solutions and encourage parents to do this as well.

TOOL

Tool 2 provides more information about solution-focused meetings and a sample meeting planner.

## Home–School Communication

There are many ways for school staff and parents to communicate including

- regular phone calls and e-mails
- informal visits and check-ins
- scheduled conferences and meetings
- home–school communication books

When parents and school staff feel it would be beneficial to maintain regular and frequent home–school communication, they may choose to set up a daily or weekly communication book. It is important that parents and staff work collaboratively to decide what these communication systems should focus on and how they will be maintained. Ideally, communication should focus on the identified academic and social behaviour goals that the student is working on. This system should be a way to share good news between school and home.

Writing anecdotal notes to parents at the end of a busy school day can be difficult for school staff to manage, particularly if there are a number of students using this communication system. Writing unstructured ad-hoc notes can also deliver inconsistent messages. They may unintentionally overemphasize a single behaviour and/or under-report positive behaviour.

Checklists with scaled indicators of how the student demonstrated a certain observable behaviour at different times of the school day are the easiest to maintain and the most direct way to communicate (sample indicators: consistently, some of the time, seldom, not at all).

The behaviour descriptions and data should be written in parent-friendly (and student-friendly) language. These checklists can provide useful feedback to students and can include a self-reflection component that encourages students to evaluate and report on their own behaviour for the day.

TOOL

Tool 3: Home–School Communication Book provides a sample template for a communication book.

It is important to develop strategies to make the communication system as stress-free as possible for the student, family, and school staff. Students may need special reminder systems to bring the book back and forth between home and school, or technology such as e-mail may offer some innovative solutions. In addition, students and their family's privacy must be protected so no confidential or potentially embarrassing or damaging information should be recorded in the book. The tone should be positive and it should be a way that family and school staff can work together to support and encourage the student.

For resources about home–school communication, refer to our Web site: www.pearsoncanada.ca/ci

## Strengthen Peer Relationships

Students with behaviour disabilities often have difficulty forming positive relationships with peers because they may lack the social skills necessary to negotiate and mediate friendships. They also tend to form relationships with others who have similar behaviour difficulties and this increases the social challenges of peer relationships.

### Sample Strategies for Developing Peer Relationships

- Encourage small groups of students to work collaboratively on specific projects, and help them to understand and practise the different roles involved in effective group work.
- Involve student in games and other recreational activities (with adult supervision and support).
- Use role-playing to teach alternative responses to social difficulties or conflicts among peers.
- Set up guidelines or develop a menu of strategies for resolving conflicts for students who have social difficulties. These supports can help them begin to work out minor difficulties between themselves.
- Group students strategically. Look for combinations of students who can work well together.

- Provide adequate supervision during group work to ensure positive behaviour is reinforced and to intervene quickly if bullying or other problem behaviours occur.

## Use Reframing Instead of Criticism

Look for opportunities to show students a new picture of themselves. Instead of pointing out what's wrong, describe what's right and what still needs to be done.

Intentionally use positive descriptions rather than negative descriptions. In *Raising Your Spirited Child* (1991), Mary Sheedy Kurcinka contrasts negative descriptions with positive descriptions. For example,

| Negative Descriptions | Positive Descriptions |
|---|---|
| Demanding | Has high standards |
| Loud | Enthusiastic |
| Argumentative | Opinionated, strongly committed to goals |
| Nosy | Curious |
| Wild | Energetic |
| Explosive | Dramatic |
| Distractible | Perceptive |

To rename and reframe with positive language, here are four simple steps.

1. Think of a student with problem behaviour.
2. Rename one or more of his or her negative traits as positive traits.

   Examples: stubbornness = determination
   talking back = honesty
   constant movement = energy
3. Identify the positive traits you want to encourage the student to practise.
4. Put into a positive sentence.

Examples: With a student who tends to talk back: "Mattais, I appreciate your honesty in stating your opinion. How can you make your point in a more respectful way?" With an active, restless student: "Havla, you have great energy. Now you need to turn that energy on your social studies project and finish up that chart."

This kind of reframing can help students change their mental pictures of themselves and their power to influence situations.

## Teach Positive Self-Talk

Students with behaviour disabilities often use the kind of self-talk after a confrontation or adversarial situation that further supports their already negative view of themselves. They may think, "Oh, what an idiot," or "Why did I say that? How stupid can I be?"

Provide explicit and systematic instruction about replacing negative self-talk with positive self-talk. For example:

- Teach examples of positive self-talk statements: "I did that well," "I tried that task," "I recognized that Sue calling me a name was a trigger for me so I did a great job of walking away," or "I made a mistake but it's just a mistake so I need to keep calm."
- When teaching and practising new or replacement behaviour, prompt students to use positive self-talk.
- Prompt students to use positive self-talk in relevant situations throughout the school day.
- Model positive self-talk with comments such as, "I did a great job on that chart," "Mistakes are hard for me but I'm willing to try something new," "We all make mistakes—now, what can I learn from this?"
- Point out examples of other people using positive self-talk, especially popular peers, favourite adults, or sports heroes.

# Modification of the Classroom Environment

2

> "Students need structure to give them the message that the classroom is a safe, predictable place where learning happens."
>
> – Robert Marzano, Senior Scholar,
> Mid-continent Research for Education and Learning

The structure of the physical school and classroom environment contributes to effective educational programming and support for students with behaviour disabilities. A thoughtfully structured physical environment is also beneficial for other students. A safe, orderly, calm, flexible, and efficient classroom environment makes instruction and learning more effective.

Begin by conducting an environmental scan to assess the physical set-up of the classroom and how it might affect learning and behaviour.

TOOL

Tool 4: Environmental Classroom Scan provides advice about assessing the classroom's physical set-up.

## Sample Strategies for Creating a Calm, Quiet Physical Environment

- *Reduce the noise level.*
  Use carpeting on the floor, or a portion of the floor, or put tennis balls or carpet pieces on the ends of the legs of desks or chairs.
- *Assess the soundscape of the classroom.*
  Note bothersome noises and take steps to reduce them; for example, buzzing or humming lights and heating pipes, the sounds of passing traffic, and noises from other classrooms.
- *Provide headphones for students to use to block sound during quiet time.*
  Some students are unable to block out background noises and are distracted by a teacher talking with another student or even a ticking clock.
- *Set a relaxing tone.*
  Try using relaxing music when students are working individually at their desks.

- *Consider furniture layout.*
  Arrange classroom furniture and partitions to create traffic patterns that discourage running and decrease students' tendencies to bother each other while they work.

- *Reduce distractions.*
  Consider using window coverings to reduce the effects of noise, temperature, light, and visual distractions.

## Make the Classroom Space Flexible

If space permits, organize the classroom into several distinct activity areas. For example, provide areas for computer use, science inquiries, art projects, and other areas devoted to specific subjects and activities. Students learn that they are to pursue specific activities in each space.

Set up separate workspaces for different tasks or different parts of the day. For example, use a table at the front of the classroom for group instruction or seatwork. Designate tables at a different location for small group work or independent work.

Use study carrels and other independent spaces as "private offices" for students. Use these carrels to limit distractions or as a place where students can go to calm down and regain their composure after behavioural outbursts. Do not associate carrels with punishment by sending students there only when they misbehave. Invite students to think about how adults often prefer to work in independent offices or workspaces.

Have students organize their personal workspaces to promote efficient learning and develop independent work habits.

### Sample Strategies for Helping Students Get Organized

- *Create individual storage areas.*
  Give students additional space near their desks (for example, a shelf or plastic tub) where they can store and organize personal belongings. Placing items at eye level may make materials easier to find and put away.

- *Put supplies in boxes.*
  Label the boxes with picture clues as well as words. Keep these boxes in the same location so students always know where to look for them. Colour code the boxes or their labels; for example, yellow for language arts and blue for math.

- *Provide boxes filled with pencils, pens, pencil crayons, scissors, glue sticks, rulers, and paper that students can borrow.*
  Students can be more independent if they can borrow some classroom supplies without asking.
- *Work collaboratively with individual students to find out what they need to organize themselves.*
  For example, ask them:
  - "How could you arrange the inside of your desk so your paper, pencil, and eraser are always close at hand?"
  - "What should you do with your homework so you can always find it quickly?"
- *Encourage students to keep track of their own materials.*
  Provide class time to label personal items and storage locations with their own names, pictures, or a personal symbol in a colour of their choice.
- *Prompt students to put away items.*
  Encourage them to place notebooks, pencils, erasers, rulers, and other materials in the same spot at the end of each activity.
- *Some students benefit from not having anything in or on their desks to distract them.*
  Empty their desks and keep the materials close at hand. Alternatively, turn the desks around so the openings face away from the students.
- *Provide quiet, nondistracting ways to "wiggle."*
  Some students find it helpful to have "fidget material" such as a sponge ball to squeeze.
- *Consider location of lockers.*
  Whenever possible, assign individual lockers (versus shared lockers) in a less-travelled location to provide easier access in a less-crowded environment.
- *Make sure the locks are easy to open.*
  Key locks may be more appropriate than combination locks. Look for new locks that use letters in a meaningful word, rather than a number combination.
- *Encourage students to keep their lockers organized.*
  Teach specific strategies such as putting books for morning classes on the bottom and afternoon books on the top. Schedule a regular weekly clean-up to keep lockers free of clutter.
- *Provide visual reminders.*
  Have students post daily schedules and monthly calendars of assignments on the inside of their locker doors.

## Provide Specialized Areas for Individual Students[2]

Students with behaviour disabilities often benefit from designated instructional areas such as

- a quiet area for one-to-one instruction with the teacher, a teacher assistant, or a peer helper
- an area where the student may go with another student to work on specific academic skills
- an area where a student and selected other students may go to play games that develop social skills

Teachers may also have these students go to a designated area as a predetermined consequence when they engage in a specific negative behaviour such as refusing to do assignments, disrupting the class, or hurting another student. For example,

- a time-away area such as a desk or table at the back of the class in clear view of the teacher or a designated area outside of the room that is supervised
- a time-out area, usually outside of the room, where the student goes after displaying a significantly problematic behaviour

Time outs should allow sufficient time to defuse the situation, but not be of such a length that the student misses important instruction. Falling behind academically can create frustration and more behavioural issues. For more information on the use of time outs, see pages 62 to 63.

Students with behaviour disabilities may need preferential seating in the classroom; for example, near the teacher or positive peer models, or at the front of the class on an outside row where there are fewer distractions. When students sit near the teacher, they can tune into cues such as eye contact and hand gestures, and the teacher can privately repeat instructions on a level the student can understand.

As much as possible, locate the student away from

- auditory and visual distractions, such as windows and things to manipulate
- other students who are easily distracted or could potentially face conflicts

---

2. Adapted with permission from Dwaine Souveny and Dianna Souveny, *ABCs for Success with Attention Deficit Disorders* (Red Deer, AB: Dynamic Networks, 2000).

## Create a Safe Place[3]

Designate a small corner of the classroom where individual students can go to relax, refocus, and reflect. This is different from a time-out space because it is a space students choose to go to and it should not be used as a negative consequence. Rather, students can use this area when they are upset or angry and need time alone to calm down and gain control of themselves.

Pick a spot in the classroom that offers some privacy but from where the student also has a clear view of the classroom. At the same time, the teacher needs to be able to clearly see who is in the Safe Place at any time.

Furnish with a soft chair and items such as a squishy ball or favourite books, or a listening centre with music that might help students calm themselves.

Introduce the concept of the Safe Place by teaching and practising a self-calming strategy such as STAR (**S**top, **T**ake a deep breath **A**nd **R**elax) and discussing the rules of using the Safe Place.

1. You can go to the Safe Place when you are angry, sad, or want to be alone.
2. Only one person at a time may be in the Safe Place.
3. If you need the Safe Place when someone is in it, you could
    - wait until he or she is out
    - ask him or her if you could have a turn
    - sit at a table near the Safe Place quietly and alone until it is available
    - use another strategy to help calm yourself

## Develop Effective Classroom Routines

Teaching a new routine requires clear and concise vocabulary, direct instruction, practice, and monitoring. This process may take from two to six weeks.

Students with behaviour disabilities may need extra assistance with the following kinds of routines:

- coming into class
- interacting with others
- requesting the teacher's attention, permission, or assistance

3. The Safe Place is part of the Conscious Discipline program. Reproduced with permission from Loving Guidance, Inc. www.ConsciousDiscipline.com 800-842-2846.

- accessing supplies or equipment
- maintaining time on task
- completing assignments
- using unstructured time
- requesting choices or alternatives
- requesting time to talk to the teacher about something personal
- knowing what to do in emergency situations such as fire drills

## Sample Strategies for Developing Effective Classroom Routines

- *Directly teach all routines.*
  "This is the way we set up for math," "Give me five means …"
- *Practise and reinforce routines frequently.*
  This is especially important at the beginning of the school year and when a new student joins the class.
- *Generate checklists for specific routines.*
  Strategically post these step-by-step explanations around the classroom—in the coatroom, in the listening corner, at the reading centre, on students' desks.
- *Encourage students to use self-talk as they follow the routines.*
  Model and practise what students should do in each routine, using pictures as well as words. Keep the routines short at first (one to three steps) and gradually add extra steps.
- *Use correction, not consequences, when teaching routines.*
  Focus on guided practice and constructive feedback to help students master new routines.
- *Encourage students to develop their own routines.*
  Help them develop sequentially ordered lists of activities and tasks they need to complete regularly; for example, getting ready to work or packing up homework.

# Differentiated Instruction

3

> "Teaching is a strategic act of engagement."
>
> – James Bellanca,
> "Teaching for Intelligence: In Search of Best Practices"

The pervasiveness and severity of their behaviour difficulties may interfere with the classroom learning and academic success of students with behaviour disabilities. As a result, they may

- miss out on many academic experiences
- lack basic academic skills and concepts
- have underdeveloped work and study skills
- have developed habits related to avoiding or escaping challenging academic tasks
- have negative attitudes toward school and learning, and view themselves as unsuccessful learners

As students' behaviour improves and stabilizes, they may need continual instructional adaptations and accommodations to support their academic learning. Effective instruction meets students at their level of performance and helps them move forward.

Differentiating instruction ensures that teachers move from teaching programs to teaching individual students. If students who have behavioural disabilities are to be successful, then instruction must be personalized and relevant. Teachers must recognize the varying interests, experiences, developmental needs, backgrounds, and cultures in their classroom. The learning environment needs to be structured so that it is flexible and engages every student. Depending on the individual needs of the students, teachers will possibly need to differentiate the content, instructional methods, and the means of assessment and evaluation. Differentiation does not mean lowering standards.

For resources about differentiated instruction, see our Web site: www.pearsoncanada.ca/ci

## Consider the Timing of Activities

Some students learn better and are more responsive in the morning; others do better in the afternoon. Try to provide more challenging tasks and activities during times when the student is more responsive, and reduce expectations and give more breaks at other times. Also, alternate less-interesting tasks with highly interesting ones. For example, the sequence could be

- read aloud with teacher
- do a short written assignment
- play a game with a partner
- revise writing assignment
- engage in physical activity

In secondary schools, balance timetables so more challenging subjects are evenly distributed across semesters.

*Behavioural momentum* involves getting a student engaged in a preferred task, then moving fairly quickly into a less preferred task while he or she is still active and in a positive state; for example, playing a game of snakes and ladders for a few minutes, then putting sight words on some of the squares to be read along the way. Use instructions that are likely to be followed quickly and easily, use brief simple requests, then change requests to less preferable requests after the student has readily responded to several.

## Teach Students Strategies for Completing Tasks

If students have difficulty completing tasks, invest some time in teaching them the necessary skills. Following is an example of a step-by-step teaching sequence.

1. Establish a "task-completion time" twice a day. Use a specific visual cue (such as a sign) that indicates this training time is about to begin.
2. Set the timer for the goal time. Begin with a duration appropriate for the student (e.g., two to 10 minutes) and then increase the time incrementally after the student has successfully completed the task within the time limit during three out of four sessions. Continue to increase the time when the student meets the criterion, until the time is comparable to the time expected of other students in the class.
3. Provide students with tasks that are appropriate for their academic skill level and that they can easily accomplish in the allotted time.
4. Provide a prearranged reinforcement for successful task completion.

5. If students do not complete the task in the allotted time, simply take the task away and give no positive reinforcement. Do not give negative consequences either, as this is simply a training and practice session. If students do not successfully complete the task in at least two out of four sessions, try to provide for success-oriented learning by reducing the time or making the task easier.

6. Praise the student for
   - doing the task (e.g., "You did a great job of matching the cities to the provinces")
   - completing the task (e.g., "You reached your goal of completing the whole page")

7. Tell the student he or she is a "task completer" when tasks are completed in the time allotted for all students.

8. When the task completion session time is within four minutes of the regular class activity time, begin phasing out the praise and rewards, using them only intermittently

# 4 Understanding Individual Student Behaviour

> "Always assume that a motivation for a particular behaviour is positive but expressed in a negative way."
>
> – Richard L. Curwin and Allen N. Mendler, *Discipline with Dignity*

To effectively support students with behaviour disabilities and to help them develop new and more positive behaviours, teachers need to understand why students behave as they do. One effective way of understanding students' problem behaviour is to recognize that the behaviour has a function. In many instances, the behaviour allows students to obtain something they want or avoid something they do not want.

The same behaviour can have different functions for different students. For example, students may hit others in order to be left alone or take something away from a classmate to get attention.

Research studies and evidence-based best practices have identified the following principles.[4] Behaviour is learned and therefore can be unlearned.

- Each student is unique and therefore requires an individualized approach based on the purpose or function of the student's behaviour.
- The first step of an intervention is to identify the purpose or function that the current behaviour serves.
- Behaviour is influenced by the types of reinforcements or other consequences received after the behaviour occurs.
- Teachers and school-based teams need observational data to determine the function of the behaviour and the effects of antecedents and consequences surrounding that behaviour.
- Teachers and school-based teams need to understand the function of behaviour in order to select appropriate teaching strategies.
- Altering the setting or environment may improve student behaviour.
- Data collection and analysis is the basis for initial decision making as well as for continuously monitoring the programming.

4. Adapted with permission from Karen Bain and Brenda Sautner, *BOATS: Behaviour, Observation, Assessment and Teaching Strategies*, 2nd ed. (Edmonton, AB: Special Education Council, The Alberta Teachers' Association, 2007), p. 4.

- Teachers and school-based teams can enhance their competency and capacity for meeting the learning needs of students with behaviour disabilities by working through a process that consists of
  - understanding and observing behaviours
  - implementing positive behaviour supports
  - matching appropriate teaching strategies to student needs

## Behaviour Is Learned

Students learn a pattern of behaviour through observation or through feedback and consequences.

### Observation

Individuals may learn new behaviours by observing other people's behaviour, that is, through social learning or modelling. They see other people behaving in a certain way and imitate them. For example, Mary hears that the teacher excused other students for not handing in homework because they claimed to have forgotten it at home. So she uses a similar excuse. Or Barry's parents encourage hitting as a way of "standing up for yourself." So Barry responds to frustration with peers by physically lashing out.

### Feedback and Consequences

Students learn behaviours through the feedback and consequences they receive at home or school. Sometimes feedback or consequences unintentionally reinforce negative behaviours. For example, a teacher responds to a student who frequently calls out in class by giving him more attention, which is what he wants. Or students try to get sent out of class for disrupting the class in order to avoid a task or activity they dislike.

## Functions of Behaviour

All behaviour has a function. Often the function is to

- obtain something (such as attention, activities, goods, or control)
- avoid something (such as specific activities or social situations)

In addition, low tolerance for frustration may also contribute to problem behaviour.

### Obtaining Something

- Some people require very little attention from others while others require a great deal. Students who are unable to obtain attention in appropriate ways may resort to negative behaviours such as calling out in class, disrupting or hitting other students, or swearing.
- Students may become aggressive in order to obtain desired goods from other students.
- Students may intentionally display oppositional behaviour to gain control over their environment.

### Avoiding Something

- Students who do not like attention, or at least certain types of attention, act out or refuse to participate in order to avoid that attention.
- Students may display inappropriate behaviour in class to avoid doing a task or answering a question when they don't know the answer. They are more concerned about not looking "stupid" or "dumb" than about the consequences of their behaviour. Being disruptive sometimes gets them out of the class so they can avoid the situation for a while.
- Students may lie or cheat to avoid the unpleasant consequences of their negative behaviour.

## Trigger Events

In many cases, an event triggers an emotional reaction or problem behaviour.

Typical "fast" triggers in the immediate environment include

- being asked to do something
- being told "no"
- receiving negative feedback or a negative consequence
- being in stressful situations; for example, the teacher asks for an answer in class or the student is anxious about writing tests or being involved in large groups
- being near a person the student feels is adversarial
- perceiving that someone said something or did something that is threatening or unpleasant

- overreacting to school work the student perceives as too difficult, too complex, or irrelevant
- the teacher's absence

"Slow triggers" that may result in negative behaviour at a later time include

- family-related factors such as parental depression, family anger, ineffective parenting, separation and loss, or abuse
- medical and health issues such as lack of sleep, poor nutrition, or the effects of medication
- social and community factors such as peer groups (including gangs) or extracurricular activities or a part-time job

It can be difficult to identify the trigger event if you don't understand the student's past history or present developmental characteristics. Teachers might try asking the student to recall what he or she was thinking or feeling before becoming upset, but the student may not be able to respond in any helpful way.

While the trigger may not be easily recognizable because it stems from

- built-up frustration as the day progresses, resulting in increased fidgetiness, self-stimulation, or covering the ears or eyes,
- specific sights, sounds, or smells that the student finds irritating (e.g., loud noises such as a fire alarm or smells), or
- sounds or smells that bring back memories of trauma such as abuse,

Teachers must suspend judgment and not conclude that any one factor caused the behaviour. The complex interrelationship of factors negates simplistic interpretations.

## The Escalation Cycle

Some students have difficulty recognizing the events that trigger their problem behaviour and therefore have a limited ability to prevent their behaviour from escalating. Others may be able to recognize the escalation cycle but still choose to engage in inappropriate behaviour. School staff need to understand the escalation cycle and develop skills for dealing with volatile situations proactively.

## The Escalation Cycle[5]

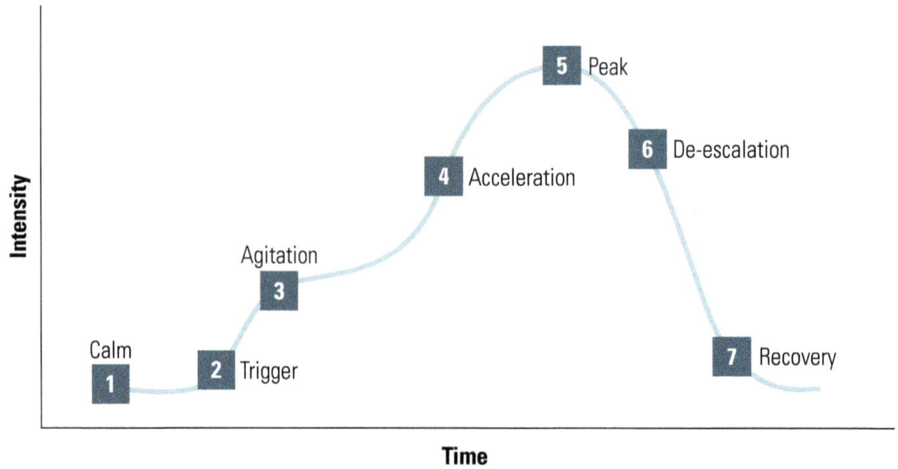


The best time to teach new or replacement behaviour is when the student is in the calm phase of the cycle. Students can practise this behaviour through role-playing and then use it in actual situations.

## Sample Strategies for De-escalating Conflict Situations

- *Use brief, simple stress-reduction techniques before responding to a student's remark or behaviour.*
  For example, take a deeper-than-normal breath and release it slowly. As an added benefit, this technique creates an additional moment to plan an appropriate response.

- *Respond to the student in a neutral, business-like, calm voice.*
  People often interpret their own emotional states from their own behavioural cues. Speaking calmly is more likely to help you believe that you are calm (and act like you are calm)—even when you are in the midst of a stressful situation.

- *Keep responses brief.*
  Short responses give students less control over the interaction and can also prevent you from inadvertently rewarding negative behaviour with too much attention.

- *Use well-timed, supportive techniques to interrupt the escalation of student anger.*
  These types of tactics can redirect a potential confrontation into a productive conversation. Interrupting tactics should be positive and respectful; for example, they can divert students' attention from conflict by redirecting their attention to more positive topics or activities.

5. Reproduced with permission from Geoff Colvin, *Managing the Cycle of Acting-Out Behavior in the Classroom* (Eugene, OR: Behavior Associates, 2004), Figure 2.1, p. 12.

- *Try paraphrasing the essential points of the student's concerns.*
  Many students lack effective negotiation skills in dealing with adults. As a result, these students may become angry and defensive when they try to express a complaint to school staff—even when that complaint is well founded. Show that you want to understand the student's concern by summing up the crucial points of that concern, using the student's own words. Use phrases such as, "Let me be sure that I understand you correctly …", "Are you telling me that …?", "It sounds to me like your concerns are …" Engaging in active listening by using paraphrasing demonstrates respect for the students' points of view and can also help improve their own understanding of the problem.

- *Use open-ended questions to better understand the problem situation and find possible solutions.*
  Pose who, what, where, when, and how questions such as "What do you think made you angry when you were talking with Sam?" and "Where were you when you realized that you had misplaced your science book?" In general, avoid asking "why" questions because the student can perceive this as blaming (e.g., "Why did you get into that fight with Jerry?"). Some students may become even more frustrated when asked "why" questions because they may not be able to answer them.

- *Use nonverbal strategies to defuse potential confrontations.*
  When people get into arguments, they often unconsciously mirror the emotional posturing of the other. For example, pointing when the other person points, standing when the other person stands, and so on. To lower the tension when a student is visibly agitated, sit down next to the student (a less threatening posture) rather than standing over that student.

- *Ask the student, "Is there anything that we can work out at this time to earn your cooperation?"*
  Such a statement treats the student with dignity, models negotiation as a positive means for resolving conflict, and demonstrates that you want to keep the student in the classroom. It also provides the student with a final chance to resolve the conflict and avoid other, more serious consequences. When asked this type of question, students will often come up with good ideas for resolving the problem.

## Dealing with Aggressive and Destructive Behaviour

Individual students may occasionally become aggressive and refuse to de-escalate their behaviour or remove themselves from a situation. This means the current level of support and intervention needs to be intensified or altered in some way. In the meantime, school jurisdictions need policies and procedures for responding when students threaten or place themselves or others at risk. Ideally, these procedures are individualized to accommodate the behavioural profile of specific students whose history suggests that they are at risk of becoming aggressive.

To ensure the safety of all individuals in the school, the teacher and other school staff need to

- develop an individual behaviour support plan that systematically addresses the behaviours of concern (see pages 75 to 83)
- focus on prevention and on developing positive behaviours to replace problem behaviours
- plan how to address situations that might put individual students or their peers at risk (e.g., removing the student or removing the other students from the situation)
- provide relevant training for staff who are involved and require them to use nonviolent crisis intervention
- include a communications component in individual behaviour support plans and ensure that this plan provides for
  - classroom staff having direct communication with administrative staff (e.g., intercom or cell phones), with specific communication codes for the type of assistance they need
  - a communication strategy for informing parents about what has occurred

## Social Factors

Some students develop challenging behaviours because of things that are happening at home or in their community. These situations are generally beyond the influence of the school. It is often neither possible nor appropriate (because of confidentiality issues) for all school staff working with a student to have specific information about family-related circumstances. However, when trying to understand and empathize with students' behaviour disabilities, staff may find it useful to generally consider how family and community factors can affect student behaviour.

Family factors may include

- who is living in the home such as parents, partners, siblings, extended family
- siblings, birth order, and potential rivalries
- the stability of home life
- employment situations; for example, one or both parents working out of town for extended periods
- family stressors such as addictions or financial difficulties

- availability of family support; for example, having lunches made or getting help with homework
- recent traumatic events such as death, divorce, or separation
- parental discipline and structure, or lack of it, in the home
- parents' and family members' physical and mental health; for example, depression or serious injuries

Community factors include

- peer groups: who they are and whether they share common interests with the student
- availability of extracurricular activities
- supervision within the community
- stability of the community
- drug or alcohol abuse
- cultural factors such as ethnic issues

## Bullying Behaviour

Recent research by Tanya Beran (2005) at the University of Calgary looked at the relationship between bullying and behaviour problems. Beran found that students who regularly and frequently intimidate, threaten, and harass their peers experience significantly more behaviour problems than students who bully less often. Frequent bullying behaviour is associated with other types of overt behaviours including

- disrupting others
- instigating fights
- becoming easily angered
- resisting following rules

Moreover, students who frequently bully are less likely to accept responsibility for problems they are involved in, and are more likely to perceive the other person involved as "causing the problem" or "deserving it."

Other social-emotional issues associated with students who bully include

- depression
- anxiety
- fear
- social skills difficulties

School-related difficulties associated with this group of students include

- poor concentration
- low achievement
- absenteeism

## Functions of Bullying Behaviour

It is possible that students who bully frequently do so for different reasons than students who bully infrequently. Students who engage in continual bullying may be preoccupied with the need to

- control
- obtain attention
- win in all peer interactions

Through positive reinforcement provided by the attention of bystanders, bullying behaviours may be maintained and increased. This behaviour may also be related to depression, perhaps in realization that peers may show respect toward them in the form of fear, but may not particularly like them. Students who bully their peers may not feel a sense of belonging at school and this can be aggravated by additional difficulties with learning, attention, and adaptive skills.

In contrast, students who do not demonstrate bullying behaviour tend to have stronger social and learning skills and have learned the negotiation and mediation skills essential for adapting successfully in social and academic situations.

## Interventions to Reduce Bullying Behaviour

Students who frequently bully need targeted coaching to learn alternatives to aggressive behaviours. They also need more intensive kinds of support such as coping and friendship skills training and family support. Bullying prevention approaches that provide information about the harm of bullying will be ineffective for these students who bully frequently. Rather, these students will require intensive individualized support to help them improve their social skills and emotional regulation.

For resources about bullying prevention and intervention, see our Web site: www.pearsoncanada.ca/ci

Bullying has become an issue of concern across the globe, resulting in the adoption of prevention and intervention strategies. Schools recognize that they cannot solve these issues alone; therefore, school systems include the broader community stakeholders in addressing the issue. For these initiatives to be successful, student engagement is essential in the development, implementation, and review of policies, practices, and strategies.

The primary focus must be on prevention, followed by consistent intervention. School systems also need to communicate clearly that there are consequences for bullying behaviour. It is important for all students to feel safe within the learning environment, and for parents to have confidence in the school's management of behavioural issues.

## Neurological Factors

Some students display challenging behaviour because they do not have the knowledge or skills they need to behave more positively. These students may not know how to meet behavioural expectations, or have difficulty meeting them, because they have neurologically based disabilities such as learning disabilities, attention deficit/hyperactivity disorder (AD/HD), fetal alcohol spectrum disorder (FASD), autism spectrum disorders, or mental illness.

To better understand how students' disabilities can affect their learning and behaviour, refer to the resources on our Web site: www.pearsoncanada.ca/ci

## Using a Functional Behavioural Assessment (FBA) Approach

A **functional behavioural assessment (FBA)** is an effective process to gather data to identify problem behaviours and examine[6]

- the relationship between events in the environment
- what comes before and after problem behaviours
- the occurrence or nonoccurrence of specified behaviours under particular circumstances

A functional behavioural assessment does not end with data collection. The data collected must be used to develop a behaviour support plan that will increase positive behaviour, teach new replacement behaviours, and reduce or eliminate problem behaviour. An FBA is not complete until a behaviour support plan is in place and is working effectively.

The presence of a variety of environmental influences can predict, cause, prevent, and/or maintain both problem behaviours and appropriate behaviours. A functional behavioural assessment provides information necessary for selecting appropriate interventions for modifying problem behaviours and teaching socially appropriate replacement skills.

6. This section is adapted with permission from Karen Bain and Brenda Sautner, *BOATS: Behaviour, Observation, Assessment and Teaching Strategies*, 2nd ed. (Edmonton, AB: Special Education Council, The Alberta Teachers' Association, 2007), pp. 40–44.

The assessment involves gathering information by a variety of methods, including interviews, rating scales, and systematic observation.

Direct observations of an individual student in natural environments under a range of conditions are challenging to complete, but will result in richer data. Sometimes, after observations, it may be helpful to experiment with factors. This can be done by carefully manipulating antecedents and/or consequences of problem behaviours to verify their influence on the problem behaviour.

Use the results of observations to identify the purpose of the problem behaviour. The observational data should identify the environmental situations most likely to be in place when problem behaviours occur, and identify the reinforcement the individual is currently receiving for those behaviours. To teach new and more appropriate behaviours, it is important to select positive replacement behaviours which will serve the same function and offer similar kinds of positive reinforcement. For example, if teacher attention has been identified as inadvertently reinforcing shouting out, teach students to raise hands to gain that attention.

Understanding the consequences and functions that maintain problem behaviours is just the starting point. The assessment must also provide details about the physical and social environment that sets the occasion for problem behaviour so that school staff can modify the environment in ways that directly lead to more positive behaviours. The outcome of an effective behavioural assessment should be an individual behaviour support plan that aligns with a student's individualized education or program plan (IEP/IPP).

To perform a functional behavioural assessment:

1. Establish **data-collecting procedures** for direct observation such as forms to record frequency, duration, interval, and anecdotal information. A common tool for doing this is an ABC chart, in which "A" refers to the Antecedents of "B" the Behaviour, and "C" the Consequences of the behaviour (see chart on next page). Ensure that all people collecting information understand the procedures to be used.

   Other methods of collecting data about behaviour include

   - **event recording**: notes the number of times one behaviour occurs within a set time
   - **interval recording**: identifies behaviour patterns by recording behaviours occurring within a set time
   - **momentary time sampling**: notes whether a behaviour occurs at a specific time
   - **duration recording**: records the length of time a specific behaviour lasts

   For more information about these methods, see pages 69 to 74.

TOOL

Tool 5 provides a sample template for observing and recording behaviour.

| Antecedents | Behaviour | Consequences |
|---|---|---|
| **Fast triggers:**<br>• teasing by classmates<br>• timed tests<br>• tasks involving a considerable amount of writing<br>• open-ended writing or thinking activities<br>• receiving less-than-perfect marks<br><br>**Slow triggers:**<br>• lack of organizational skills<br>• lack of impulse control<br>• inability to read social situations<br>• difficulty with abstract or metaphorical language<br>• lack of fine motor skills | • becomes verbally abusive<br>– screams obscenities<br>– threatens to harm others<br>• refuses to complete work<br>• walks out of class | • warning from teacher<br>• increased teasing by peers<br>• removal from classroom/school<br>• one-on-one talks with teacher/teaching assistant/other school staff/administrator<br>• tasks are not completed |

2. Use collected data to **identify** what specific behaviours require change. Assess behaviours interfering with safety, and academic and social success. Focus on behaviours that have long-term significance as well as immediate concerns. It is most essential to change behaviours that involve aggression or self-injury, or that are socially stigmatizing. Rank behaviours in terms of their need for change. Consider the extent and frequency of behaviours and use this data to set the priorities for the plan.

3. Ensure these **behaviours** have clear definitions and can be understood by any staff working with the student as well as by parents and other caregivers.

4. Identify physiological, psychological, environmental, and social **factors contributing** to **problem behaviours**. Identify or predict times, events, demands, or environmental conditions during which the problem behaviour frequently or always occurs.

   These contributing factors may include task demands, people in the environment, medications, seizure activity, staff changes, and/or daily activities, any of which can influence behaviour. These events "set the occasion" for behaviours—they are the **antecedents** of the behaviour. Some antecedents occur immediately prior to the behaviour. Other

TOOL

Tool 6 provides a tool for recording answers to questions about a specific problem behaviour.

events may contribute to problem behaviour, but be less connected in time. Reinforcement may be more or less important at certain times; for example, food may be highly reinforcing after five hours of no food, but may not be reinforcing directly following a meal.

5. Identify physiological, psychological, environmental, and social **factors contributing** to **appropriate, socially successful behaviour**. Identify or predict times, events, demands, or environmental conditions during which the problem behaviour rarely or never occurs.

6. Use a **collaborative assessment** and planning approach with people who know the student best. This approach may involve an interview with the student's school team members and, when possible, an interview with the student.

   Use checklists or behaviour charts specifically related to direct observation in a particular setting. Assess behaviours across settings, people, and tasks. If possible, collect at least five days of observation.

7. Analyze data to identify the **functions** the behaviour is serving the student. Identify the consequences currently maintaining the behaviour—what the individual is "getting out of." Often the student is communicating wants and needs; however, the function may be more than one type. The following are commonly identified functions of problem behaviours. One behaviour may also serve more than one function.

   Typical functions include

   a. escape from demands

   b. escape from activities

   c. escape from particular people

   d. attention

   e. access to preferred objects or activities

   f. relief of stress or anxiety

   g. increase or decrease in sensory stimulation

   h. self-stimulation

   i. automatic behaviour and habits

   The function of the behaviour will help identify the most effective type of intervention to change that behaviour. The following chart illustrates typical functions of behaviour and possible interventions.[7]

7. Chart on page 39 adapted with permission from Jeffrey Sprague et al., *Best Behavior: Building Positive Behavior Support in Schools–Participant Training Manual (Preliminary Edition)* (Eugene, OR: Institute on Violence and Destructive Behavior, University of Oregon, 2003), Section 14, p. 4.

| Function of Behaviour | Possible Interventions |
|---|---|
| Escape or avoid unpleasant activities, tasks, or persons | • reinforce student for compliance to instructions<br>• teach student how to seek help<br>• teach acceptable alternatives to escape<br>• reinforce student for absence of problem (e.g., catch them being good)<br>• initially remove or reduce demands and then gradually increase expectations |
| Attention seeking from peers or school staff | • increase attention for positive behaviours<br>• ignore problem behaviour<br>• teach acceptable alternatives for attention |
| Access to activities or tangibles | • deny access to activity or tangible<br>• teach acceptable alternatives to obtain access (e.g., ask for it politely)<br>• avoid giving access to material or activity following problem behaviour |
| Sensory stimulation | • interrupt and redirect the student<br>• use reinforcement when behaviour is not occurring<br>• increase access to alternative sources of stimulation |

8. Make **summary statements** by describing and summarizing behaviours, situations, and reinforcers that appear to be currently maintaining the problem behaviour. Identify patterns of behaviour. "During math, David rips up papers to avoid the work."

9. **Manipulate identified environmental characteristics** that appear to be influencing behaviour to prove or disprove the hypothesis if possible and if this does not provoke or escalate problem behaviour. For example, provide David only one problem per work page and allow for a few minutes of preferred activity when that one problem is completed before starting the next problem. This step can significantly reduce the frequency of the problem behaviour. Sometimes it can even prevent it altogether.

10. Set realistic and practical **behaviour change goals** that include the target replacement behaviour, conditions, and criteria for change. "David will remain seated and work 10 minutes on a math assignment."

"David will be given answers to check his own work after each five problems when the assignment appears challenging for him."

Replacement behaviours must

- be achievable within a given time frame
- be relevant to the student's needs
- be positive and enabling
- be clearly defined and understood by both students and staff[8]

### Examples

| Problem Behaviour | Replacement Behaviour |
|---|---|
| Susan wanders around the room during "O Canada." | Susan stays within a boundary around her desk. |
| Bill becomes agitated and physically strikes another child. | Bill gives the teacher an "I need a break" card. |
| Terry physically attacks one student when they are near each other. | Terry stays at least two metres away from a specific student. |

11. Design **interventions** and positive behaviour support programming which address

    - antecedents (prevention, environmental modifications, instructional adaptations to be made by staff)
    - behaviours (what replacement behaviours look like)
    - consequences (correction procedures, extra assistance, response cost, increased supervision)

    Use modelling and reinforcement to increase the effectiveness of teaching the new skill.

    Prompt and support appropriate behaviour consistently. Specify the nature and amount of positive **reinforcement** or feedback as well as correction procedures. Increase the use of reinforcement when first initiating new behaviours, then fade the reinforcement to promote greater independence and self-control.

8. Adapted with permission from Karen Bain and Brenda Sautner, *BOATS: Behaviour, Observation, Assessment and Teaching Strategies*, 2nd ed. (Edmonton, AB: Special Education Council, The Alberta Teachers' Association, 2007), p. 51.

12. Document the plan for teaching replacement behaviours. Include **what will be done** by particular staff members and make a plan about who will help and what will be different from current practices. The new replacement behaviours must serve the same function, be useful in different settings, and be easily performed.

    Identify **crisis management** strategies to be used when the student continues unsafe or destructive behaviours. Incorporate these strategies into the behaviour support plan. Collaborate with school administrators, parents, and appropriate social agencies in the development, implementation, and review of the plan.

13. Create opportunities for **generalization** of the newly learned replacement behaviours by involving different staff, different materials, and working in different settings on the same behaviours.

    **Maintain** intermittent reinforcement for newly mastered behaviour over time, especially during major transitions such as changing classrooms or schools.

14. **Evaluate** the functional behavioural assessment process as well as the targeted behaviour change. Share **results** of evaluation and data regarding behaviour as part of individualized program planning and when reviewing individual behaviour support plans. Keep written information for ongoing communication during transitions to new schools or different programs.

TOOL

Tool 7 provides a sample template for planning a functional behavioural assessment.

# 5 Social Skills Instruction

> "We shouldn't surprise students. Setting clear boundaries for acceptable and unacceptable behaviour gives students a feeling of control and predictability. Students need to know what is expected."
>
> – Barb James

Negative behaviour is often the result of a skill deficit and is not a motivational issue. Positive reinforcement and negative consequences motivate students only when they know the desired behaviour and are capable of displaying it.

Some students can readily verbalize what they are supposed to do but their actions do not correspond with their statements. Just as people who are learning to drive a vehicle with a standard transmission can often verbalize what they are supposed to do but cannot physically perform the action of shifting gears, many students require instruction and practice before they can adopt appropriate replacement behaviours.

Teaching students to manage their emotions and act appropriately and responsibly is much like teaching academic skills. Students with behaviour disabilities generally require direct and intentional teaching of targeted social skills. Additional time and support are needed for students to learn to self-regulate their emotions.

## BEHAVE Strategy

The BEHAVE strategy provides a framework for planning instruction of social skills.[9]

**B** = **Identify** the target replacement **Behaviour** or social concern:

- Collect data to assess social competency challenges.
- Select specific skill to be taught.
- State the skill objective in positive terms.
- Clarify what the student needs to know, do, and say in observable, measurable terms.

9. This strategy is adapted with permission from Karen Bain and Brenda Sautner, *BOATS: Behaviour, Observation, Assessment and Teaching Strategies*, 2nd ed. (Edmonton, AB: Special Education Council, The Alberta Teachers' Association, 2007), p. 69.

**E** = **Explain** the **Expectations**:

- List the step-by-step skill sequence required.
- Consider communication, social, and functional skill level of student.
- Communicate these behavioural expectations to staff and the student.
- Select the setting and context in which this skill is best taught—individually, small group, large group, school, or community.

**H** = **Have** clear models:

- Model the specific social skill and use clear language to describe each step.
- Use respectful and competent peers as models.

**A** = **Act** it out consistently and frequently:

- Use guided practice to learn and rehearse new skills.
- Use verbal and visual prompting to support the demonstration of the new skills.
- Create multiple opportunities to practise and master skills.
- Reinforce appropriate imitation of models.

**V** = **View** and **Value** the social skill often:

- Ensure the new social skill is more reinforcing than the inappropriate behaviour it is replacing.
- Specify how students will be reinforced and supported throughout the learning.
- Teach students to monitor their own behaviour and, if possible, reinforce themselves when they demonstrate the positive behaviour successfully.
- Provide consistent reinforcement initially, then fade.

**E** = **Expand** and **Extend** the skill:

- Communicate learning to others and expect the learning will be demonstrated elsewhere.
- Work collaboratively with parents and others across as many settings as possible.

## Teach Emotional Regulation

Some students are very quick to anger and act out verbally or physically. Other students become very anxious and engage in negative behaviours to avoid or reduce anxiety. Individuals who are depressed can react to specific situations in different ways, including self-abuse, withdrawal, or acting out.

Students who find it difficult to control their emotions benefit from having an alternative strategy to use when they are beginning to get upset. Conventional verbal cues such as "stay calm" and "relax" may be insufficient. Students with these difficulties need help to recognize the trigger event and then deal with it by means of a physical activity such as visualization or intentional breathing. The following examples provide strategies for a range of ages and developmental levels.

### Turtle Visualization Strategy

Use the turtle visualization strategy to help students replace behaviours such as withdrawal or acting out.

*Turtle Strategy*

1. Talk about a turtle. For example,
   - has strengths (it may be slow but it can still win the race with the rabbit)
   - is hard on the outside but soft on the inside
   - can go into its shell for a short time when upset and emerge feeling better

2. Demonstrate the "Do turtle" technique.
   a. Fold hands together, fingers intertwined with thumbs sticking out.
   b. Cool down by slowly blowing on each of the four legs and the head.
3. Practise the "Do turtle" technique.
   - Role-play when the student is feeling calm.
   - Next, try role-playing after a planned trigger event.
   - Cue and practise when the student is upset after a trigger event.

## SOSS Strategy

This strategy is helpful for emotional control.

> *SOSS Strategy*
>
> **S—Stop:** Understand that you need to break the circuitry and disengage.
>
> **O—Oxygenate:** Breath deeply to clear the cortisol from the brain.
>
> **S—Strengthen gratitude:** Simulate gratitude for whatever is meaningful to you to put you in a different sector of the brain.
>
> **S—Seek information:** Counter the certainty that eliminates choice and seek information about the trigger.[10]

## Body Breathing

While standing, students visualize breathing in through the soles of their feet, drawing the breath all the way up through the body and exhaling through their hands. Repeat this deep breathing exercise several times.

This strategy allows students to deep-breathe without hyperventilating. In order to breathe out through their hands, students must open their clenched fists, which helps them relax.

# Teach Students to Be Flexible and Tolerate Frustration

Teach strategies that students can use to handle difficult times.

Students can initiate the STAR strategy after a trigger event to help them stop their usual pattern of behaviour and choose new and more positive responses. (See descriptions of the STAR and SNAP strategies on the next page.)

10. The Institute for Health and Human Potential (IHHP), www.ihhp.com.

*STAR Strategy*

Teach students the STAR acronym and encourage them to use it in potentially frustrating situations or when a trigger event has occurred.

- ★ **S** – **Stop** doing what you are doing.
- ★ **T** – **Think** about something positive you should be doing.
- ★ **A** – **Act** in a way that is appropriate for the situation or **Ask** for assistance.
- ★ **R** – **Reflect** on what you have done; use self-talk to tell yourself, "Good job."

or

*SNAP Strategy*

Encourage students to use the SNAP acronym to remind themselves to use their problem-solving skills.[11]

**S** – **S**top

**N** – **N**ow

**A** – **A**nd

**P** – **P**lan

## Use Social Stories and Scripts

Social stories and scripts help students prepare for what might happen in the future.

### Social Stories[12]

Social stories are effective for students who require a high degree of structure to understand social expectations and interact successfully with others. They are simple stories that describe a social situation and how the student is expected to behave in that situation. They are especially effective with younger students and older students with developmental delays. Social stories combine language, routines, and social expectations on a personal level. They guide and direct responding and can lead to increased self-awareness and self-management. They provide a relevant, accurate orientation to a particular social context.

11. www.stopnowandplan.com

12. Adapted with permission from Karen Bain.

When developing social stories

- identify a target behaviour or problem situation which has occurred or may occur
- consider student's developmental level and use vocabulary, print size, and concepts appropriate for that student
- develop a specific step-by-step description of what the student needs to do in this situation
- consider what the student is currently doing in similar situations
- write a story using different types of sentences, including
  - **descriptive sentences** that describe the social situation and provide information
  - **directive sentences** that suggest what the student is to do (To give flexibility they often are statements such as "I will try to ..." rather than absolutes.)
  - **affirmative sentences** that are somewhat abstract, but contain stress reducers such as "this is okay" which can reassure the student (They might also include phrases such as "This is important" to cue students that this particular rule must be followed.)
  - **perspective sentences** that contain information about the internal states of other people; for example, "My sister likes ...," "Some children like ...," "My mom is happy when ..."
  - **cooperative statements** that provide information about how the student can be assisted or supported; for example, "My mom will help with ..."
- write from the student's point of view in present or future tense; for example, "I will ..."
- focus on one skill at a time
- use positive language
- answer "wh" questions: who, where, when, why, and how
- make the story concrete and literal
- use photos and pictures and, if possible, have students illustrate and/or co-write their own stories
- read and review the story with the student frequently and in different contexts
- teach the skill directly

## Social Scripts

Like a movie script, a social script details a step-by-step process of what to do or say and what another person does or says. This technique can be used with students of all ages.

Use scripts to plan for positive behaviour, or to reflect on behaviour or a situation and choose a positive option. Try to ensure that the stories describe positive behaviour. For example:

> "When I am working on math and my teacher says 'Listen,' I stop what I am doing, put down my pencil and look at her to show that I am listening."

Social scripts can also provide information about how others might view or react to the situation. For example, "When I look at the teacher to show I am listening, she smiles back at me. She likes it when students follow her directions."

Plan for new or exceptional circumstances such as school assemblies, class parties, and other potentially stressful events by developing a step-by-step social script of what will happen, what the student will do, and how others will react.

Another way of using social scripts is to write down four to 10 actions a student has taken on file cards, along with how others reacted to these actions. Use a red card to record the student's description of actions that have already occurred, and a white card to record the student's ideas about what a more positive sequence of behaviours and reactions might be. This is an effective method of reviewing what the undesirable social behaviour was and the reaction it produced. This method also helps the student plan for more appropriate behaviour and its positive consequences.

**Sample Red Card:**

I was working on my project.

Ms Teacher said "Time to shut down the computers."

I said "No."

Ms Teacher started to take me to the office.

I had a melt down and was carried to the office.

**Sample White Card:**

I was working on my project.

Ms Teacher said "Time to shut down the computers."

I said "Yes."

I will save my work and log off the computer.

☺

Ms Teacher will be happy and say thank you.

I will be happy. ☺

## Tips for Using Social Scripts

When introducing the concept, look for three to five examples of positive behaviour the student demonstrates and record these on a white card. Reinforce that students already have some of their own positive scripts.

Relate this strategy to the way actors use scripts to create television shows and movies.

Colour code the behavioural choices, using red cards for a step-by-step description of negative behaviour and white cards for a more positive script.

After the student has written the second script on the white card, rehearse it with all the students involved. Physical practice and role-play are critical.

# Teach Compliance[13]

Once expectations have been developed collaboratively with students, it is expected that students will demonstrate responsibility and self-discipline through compliance. Compliance refers to the ability and/or willingness to respond to the requests of others. Compliance and noncompliance are learned behaviours that serve a function for that individual. It is important that students be able and willing to comply with basic social expectations and basic requests, especially for safety and group inclusion purposes. For example, a young student who runs off school grounds at recess or runs off from the group during field trips creates a serious safety risk. Students need to understand and respond appropriately to basic requests such as "Stop" and "Please come here."

13. Adapted with permission from Karen Bain.

## General Tips for Teaching Compliance

1. Make sure you have the student's attention. Make eye contact (if that is appropriate for the student) and remove distractions.
2. Communicate clearly what the student needs to do. Limit the talking and use a minimum number of words to make the point. Use concrete language. Say, "Pick up the math books and please put them on the table," not the more abstract direction "Clean up."
3. Use visual cues with the verbal requests and as a follow-up reminder.
4. You can use your body to communicate, look expectant, or gesture what you want. If necessary, partial physical prompting may be useful. However, avoid physical management. Physical contact should only be used as outlined in board or district policies regarding crisis intervention. Before intervening in such a manner, you must be properly trained, and parents should be informed that certain steps for crisis management as outlined in the student's behaviour plan may be undertaken by staff.
5. If requests are not being followed, remain as neutral as possible. Do not reinforce with attention, tangible items, or discussion.
6. Try a gentle reminder of how compliance to one request will lead to being able to do a preferred activity: "First you ____ then you can ___."
7. Sometimes you may have time to "wait," but sometimes you can't. Try to avoid rushing if you know it will be a problem. Allow adequate time for completing the task.
8. Consider going ahead and doing something else rather than engaging in a power struggle. "It is time for ___, so we will have to clean up later" and return to the original request right before the next preferred activity.
9. Make sure positive reinforcements and negative consequences are clearly stated, fair, and consistently implemented. As much as possible, prevent the obtaining of preferred items or activities directly after a non-compliant act.
10. Whenever possible, use other students as positive role models.

## Variables That Affect Compliance

*Statements work better than questions.* State the expectation in the positive. "Please start your math assignment" rather than "Isn't it time to start your work?"

*"Do" requests are more desirable than "Don't" requests.* The majority of teacher requests should start behaviours rather than stop behaviours. If too many requests are to stop behaviour, then the classroom rules need to be better communicated.

*Descriptions clarify understanding.* Describe the behaviour needed. Giving specific and well-described requests will lessen confusion.

*Distance matters.* The optimal distance for making a request is about one metre away. If speaking with a smaller student, physically get down to his or her level.

*Quiet is more effective.* A soft but firm voice is more likely to inspire cooperation than a loud voice.

*Making eye contact can help focus students.* When culturally appropriate for the student, request eye contact when making a request. For example, "Jilla, please look at me. Now, I need you to …"

*Using wait time gives students time to respond.* Wait at least 10 seconds after making the request before repeating the request or giving another prompt.

*Keeping requests to a minimum increases the chances of success.* Issue a single request only twice, then follow through with a preplanned consequence. The more you request, the less likely you are to gain compliance. When beginning, make only one request at a time.

*Redirecting can help avoid power struggles.* For example, asking a student to carry something to the gym, rather than lining up for gym may be the first step in complying to requests to move from one activity to the next.

*Positive choices can encourage cooperation.* For students who are initially resistant to directions, choices rather than direct statements may be effective. For example, "Do you want to do your math on the floor or at the table?" might be more effective than the direct request "Get your math book out and get started now."

*Reinforcing natural instances of compliance can build competence.* Watch for times students are about to do something they like, then ask them to do it, and reinforce them for following through. "Thanks for ___ when I said to." Younger students can play games such as "Simon Says" and "Follow the Leader" to build positive attitudes toward compliance.

*Positive reinforcement will increase instances of compliance.* It is easy to neglect verbally or socially rewarding students for complying with a request. To get more compliance, genuinely reinforce it.

## Help Students Understand Their Own Behaviour

Students may reject behaviour support—no matter how positive—particularly if the students have oppositional characteristics. One of the most successful approaches to this problem is to collaboratively develop strategies with the student.

Students can participate in the following strategies:

- identifying the problem behaviour and becoming more aware of why it is problematic
- identifying new or replacement behaviours and why they are preferable
- identifying and agreeing to the techniques for teaching and practising the new behaviours
- identifying ways to reinforce and reward the new behaviours
- identifying negative consequences if the negative behaviour continues

## Verbal Descriptions

Try describing to students what they are doing that is inappropriate or unacceptable, and what the reactions and consequences to this negative behaviour will be. Work with the student to verbally identify and discuss the trigger events. To make this technique work, discuss what the replacement behaviours are and the reaction to expect from others (including the reinforcement). To be most effective, keep the verbal descriptions as brief as possible.

## Physical Demonstrations

Many students respond verbally to explanations but do not follow through. Address the verbal and physical aspects of students' responses, explaining that demonstration is important. For some, drawing pictures of the trigger event followed by a positive behaviour choice may be sufficient. Others need to physically demonstrate this new behaviour; for example, by role-playing.

## Modelling

Students often learn from watching and copying others' behaviour. Most teachers avoid showing that they are agitated or angry. However, if they model emotional regulation strategies such as Do Turtle or STAR, students see how these responses can be useful and effective.

## Video

Some students respond well to making a video that emphasizes the positive aspects of their social skills and shows them displaying new or replacement behaviours. The video provides a visual memory of positive behaviour.

# Positive Reinforcement

6

> "Motivation only enables us to do what we are already capable of doing."
>
> – Robert Sylwester, Emeritus Professor of Education, University of Oregon

To make positive changes, students need a clear idea of what positive behaviour is and to be positively reinforced when they demonstrate that behaviour. Positive reinforcement is any event that follows a behaviour and increases the likelihood that the behaviour will be repeated. Positive reinforcement motivates students to do what they are capable of doing.

## Intensify Reinforcement

### Vary Reinforcement

To maintain motivation and interest, vary the types of positive reinforcements that students receive. With input from students, identify positive reinforcements such as

- praise and nonverbal communication (e.g., smile, nod, thumbs up)
- social attention (e.g., a conversation, special time with the teacher or a peer)
- tangibles such as stickers, new pencils, or snacks
- activities or privileges such as playing a game, sitting in a special place in the class, drawing, writing, colouring, going to recess or gym early, having extra computer time
- secondary positive reinforcements (such as checkmarks, tokens, or certificates of recognition) for students to accumulate in order to acquire tangibles or be allowed to participate in special activities

Give these reinforcements frequently and consistently in the initial stage. They should be decreased over time to increase intrinsic motivation and self-discpline.

Some positive reinforcements are more valuable to students than others. Have students rate a list of reinforcers on a five-point scale to determine which ones they value most.

### Time the Delivery

Predetermine how frequently the positive reinforcement will be delivered. In the initial stages, students learn the behaviour–reinforcement relationship most effectively when the reinforcement is delivered consistently every time the behaviour occurs.

Strive to deliver the reinforcement immediately after the behaviour occurs. If this is not physically possible, then immediately let the student know that he or she has displayed the desired behaviour and positive reinforcement will be forthcoming. Deliver the reinforcement with enthusiasm.

## Be Sensitive to Individual Needs

Be sensitive about when and how the reinforcement is delivered. Classrooms and groups of students have their own culture. Grade 3 students may relish receiving praise that all of the other students can hear; Grade 7 students may prefer to receive positive feedback quietly; for example, a sign, gesture, or note. They may even feel that verbal praise the rest of the class can hear is a negative consequence.

To sustain the behaviour without having to deliver reinforcement every time, use a fixed ratio of delivering reinforcements to establish the new behaviour and then a variable ratio to encourage durability of the behaviour.

- **Fixed ratio**: deliver the reinforcement every second, third, or fourth time the desired behaviour occurs.
- **Variable ratio** (sometimes referred to as **intermittent scheduling**): deliver the reinforcement on an average of every fourth time the desired behaviour occurs (sometimes after the third time, sometimes after the fifth).

## Help Students Learn to Accept Positive Reinforcement

Some students may desire positive reinforcement but not know how to react when they receive it. Some students reject praise because they have a low opinion of themselves, possibly because of a history of failure or abuse.

Some students have a history of receiving "sandwiched praise," that is, praise is given, but in between mostly negative feedback. For example, an adult might say, "That is great printing, but why couldn't you do that earlier when I first asked you?" If this occurs frequently, positive reinforcement becomes an indicator for the student that something negative is going to happen.

"Drop praise" is effective in these situations. When students are demonstrating positive behaviour, walk by and quickly "drop" the praise, walking away before they have a chance to deny or argue against it. If students do try to deny it, either ignore the remarks or simply say, "That's the way that I see it."

### Verbal Praise

Verbal reinforcement is one of the most effective types of positive reinforcement that school staff can use.

*Describe the positive behaviour while giving praise.*
The comments should focus on what the student did right and be stated in positive language. For example, "That was a wonderful paragraph you wrote because ..."

*Give praise immediately.*
The sooner the positive reinforcement is given in relation to a behaviour, the more likely the student will continue or repeat that behaviour.

*Vary the statements given as praise.*
When students hear the same praise statement repeated over and over, it may lose its value.

*Provide information to students about their competence or the value of their accomplishments.*
For example, "That was a wonderful paragraph you wrote because ..." or "That was a kind thing to do when you helped Ms. Fisher carry those bags. I know it made her feel more welcome in our school."

*Attribute success to effort and ability.*
This implies that similar successes can be expected in the future. For example: "Your studying really paid off. That's a good mark on your math test. It shows you really nailed problem solving." This kind of praise also helps students gain a better appreciation of their own skills.

## Start Where the Students Are

Ensure there are plenty of opportunities for students to earn positive reinforcement. Behaviour modification programming often fails because of insufficient positive reinforcement for positive behaviours. If a student is not receiving positive reinforcement or is receiving it very infrequently, the programming is at fault. Students need to receive repeated positive reinforcement as motivation for demonstrating appropriate behaviour.

### Maintain a 4:1 Ratio

Give positive reinforcement at least four times for every one negative or corrective interaction. Success in this regard depends substantially on the initial observation and data collection. For example, if students physically strike out twice a day on average, aim to give them positive reinforcement for the replacement behaviour (e.g., keeping hands to themselves or not striking out) eight times per day. This might mean giving positive reinforcement every hour that they do not strike out.

### Create Opportunities for Success

If a student can currently only stay on task for two minutes, start by giving him or her positive reinforcement after two minutes. Then ask the student to progressively increase the amount of time on task, and give positive reinforcement accordingly. If the focus is on the student listening to the teacher and cooperating, the teacher aims to make requests that the student is likely to complete.

## Token Economies[14]

Token economies can be an integral part of creating a positive learning environment. They can increase the frequency of positive behaviours by awarding individual students with a "token" contingent on following rules or performing specific behaviours. Tokens may be coins, points on a card, checkmarks, stickers, or paper awards having an assigned value. These tokens are then exchanged at a later time for something of value to that student. Tokens may be "cashed-in" for "back-up" reinforcers such as food, objects, activities, or special privileges.

Token economies can

- lead to increased consistency of reinforcement and attention to positive behaviours
- increase motivation
- offer portability and availability across settings
- offer immediate, positive feedback and prompts without disruption to instruction task
- change or increase performance criteria as students grow more capable
- be used to teach delayed gratification

14. Adapted with permission from Karen Bain.

- be generalized to other settings, and support home programs and parent involvement
- be paired with social recognition and praise to teach the value of natural outcomes and the language of praise
- enhance rule following
- promote imitation of appropriate behaviour by observing reinforcement received by peers
- teach the language of self-evaluation and self-reinforcement

To be effective, token economies must be planned carefully. Establishing a token economy involves

- assessing students to find out if they have the ability and skills necessary to demonstrate the specific behaviours that will earn tokens
- selecting and defining specific social or academic behaviours, skills, or performance levels which require increased positive reinforcement
- selecting tokens that are easy to use and match student interests
- selecting a variety of reinforcers that reflect students' interests and preferences
- establishing a set of rules for how the tokens are provided, and for when and how tokens can be spent
- specifying how the system will be introduced and taught to students
- deciding how tokens will be managed
- training staff on
  - how and when to reinforce and how much reinforcement to give
  - use of descriptive praise to pair with tokens, "Sitting quietly—2 points!"
- deciding how data on the target behaviours will be collected and monitored over time
- planning how the behaviours will be generalized to other settings, or with other people
- specifying how the program will be faded out or new behaviours for change will be selected

## The Rainbow Friend's Club: A Social Relationship-Based Token Economy

Although many token economies are set up for individual students, group token economies can be useful for teaching rules, developing social skills, and defining social expectations in classrooms. The Rainbow Friend's Club is an example of a classroom-based token economy designed to build social skills and enhance cooperative group work in an elementary setting.

The Rainbow Store, a display on a classroom wall, held a wide variety of food, small toys, and art supplies, and cards with activities such as "10 minutes free time," or "make a cup of hot chocolate." Each item had a price tag of a certain number of points.

All students in the class had a membership card and they each selected an item from the store to work for. The students put their cards on the item they had selected and recorded their checkmarks on a score card containing a number of blanks equal to the price of their chosen item.

Checkmarks were given for specific, appropriate behaviours and this was paired with verbal praise clearly describing why the student was receiving a checkmark, "Good looking at Jeff when he talks." This descriptive feedback was particularly important at the beginning of the program as students learned the language necessary for evaluating and reinforcing their own behaviour. Checkmarks were also given to the whole group to help develop social relationships. "Everyone helped clean up, so the whole club gets a checkmark." "Wow, everyone worked together to be on time for math!"

Unless direct group instruction was taking place, as soon as the last checkmark was earned, a student could get the selected item from the store. If the last checkmark happened during the middle of an instructional task, the student waited until the first natural break to get the item—usually not more than 10 or 15 minutes. The student then selected a new item to work toward.

The class was encouraged to recognize individual students when they "got to the store" as a form of additional social praise. A meeting of The Rainbow Friend's Club was scheduled for each Friday afternoon for the last few minutes of the day. New items were displayed in the store, specific social skills were reviewed, and students who had met specific goals were recognized.

Parents were introduced to the club and the token economy, and they often contributed items to the store. As much as possible, students were involved in maintaining the store, taking care of check sheets and recording.

Students were taught to self-reinforce when a random interval buzzer was set during some work periods and at the sound of the buzzer, students would decide if they were "on task" and, if so, could give themselves a checkmark. This approach promoted personal responsibility and reflection. On occasion, students were also prompted to give other students checkmarks. "Look around and give a checkmark to someone who is staying in his or her work area and working with math blocks." This technique was instrumental in building group relationships and using the positive behaviour of others as a visual model.

# Fair and Predictable Consequences

7

> "The guiding principle for disciplinary interventions is that they should include a healthy balance between negative consequences for inappropriate behaviour and positive consequences for appropriate behaviour."
>
> – Robert Marzano, *Classroom Management That Works*

Negative consequences are designed to influence an individual to avoid a problem behaviour. However, consequences that are not perceived as fair or are not delivered consistently, can become punishing.

## Choose Effective Consequences

Teachers often select consequences that are effective in dealing with a "typical" child. For example, for the many students who prefer to be in the classroom working with others, sending them out in the hall or to the principal's office is a negative consequence. However, some students may prefer to leave the class and sit in the hall, either to be alone or to avoid doing an assignment. So in such cases a teacher who delivers this consequence is inadvertently reinforcing the problem behaviour.

For some students, any kind of attention is better than none at all. In these cases, negative consequences that give the student attention tend to reinforce problem behaviour.

Some typical positive reinforcement approaches are not effective for students with behaviour disabilities. These students might respond to praise, for example, by refusing it and then doing the opposite behaviour. Sometimes they even find praise upsetting. For example, Ms. Smith tells Robert he is printing well. He says, "I am not" and starts to scribble across the page.

## Identify the Least Restrictive or Aversive Consequence

The most successful method of facilitating long-term behavioural change is to

- use positive strategies that focus on increasing the students' competence
- make necessary accommodations to physical settings, materials, and instruction

Teachers have to plan consequences for negative behaviours in order to maintain order and safety in the classroom, but they should never implement these consequence-based interventions in isolation. There should also be complementary reinforcement strategies that motivate students to refrain from negative behaviour and demonstrate new or replacement behaviour.

### Tips for Using Negative Consequences

- Never implement negative consequences until it is clear that positive reinforcement is ineffective. Document the effectiveness (or noneffectiveness) of all behavioural methods to justify the use of alternative measures.
- Always design and implement interventions that are safe for students and staff, and that respect the students' dignity and basic rights.
- Always include parents in discussions and decisions about using negative consequences.

All school staff involved in providing positive behaviour supports have to be prepared to react to specific behaviours in consistent ways and with the same consequences. Staff responsible for carrying out behaviour support plans require skills and knowledge about behavioural principles. In middle and high schools, students may have several teachers for different subjects. It is critical that a student's teachers work together to ensure consistency in behavioural expectations, positive reinforcement, and the implementation of consequences. This understanding is emphasized by Curwin et al. (2008):

> When students perceive consequences as random, they begin to doubt that they can influence their future. ... Students will not make good choices if they cannot anticipate what the results of those choices will be.

Types of negative consequences include

- planned ignoring
- correction and overcorrection
- restitution

- response cost
- time away
- time out

## Planned Ignoring

If getting attention is the motivation for a student's behaviour, the teacher's reaction may actually encourage it. Teachers may need to teach students how to get attention in appropriate ways.

Ignoring may be difficult to implement in the classroom, particularly if the behaviour is disruptive to learning. Be aware as well that others (for example, peers) may be inadvertently reinforcing students.

As well, staff may be concerned that others think they are "not doing anything" when they choose to ignore problem behaviour. Some behavioural experts use the term "active ignoring" or "planned ignoring" to stress that this strategy takes a lot of intention and effort.

Another difficulty with planned ignoring is that an attention-seeking student may respond by increasing the frequency, intensity, or duration of the behaviour, or choose to engage in an even more problematic behaviour. Be prepared for the problem behaviour to escalate before it decreases.

## Correction

Requiring the student to correctly display the desired behaviour can be an effective consequence. For example, if students run down the hall, have them return and walk instead. Give them an opportunity to "do it right."

## Restitution

Restitution involves having the student correct the situation. For example, if he or she breaks something, ask him or her to repair it or pay for the cost of replacing it. However, educators must be sensitive to students who do not have the financial means to pay for an item they have broken. Having the student "work off" the cost by doing chores or community service may be a viable alternative. In determining such consequences, teachers must be sensitive to cultural norms, beliefs, and student dignity by consulting with parents.

## Response Cost

A response cost technique involves taking away a reward when problem behaviour is observed; for example, fines or a loss of privileges. Response costs must be immediate and consistent, not spontaneously determined. If not properly implemented, the response cost technique can escalate problem behaviour, as students may feel they have nothing to lose. Also, some students can become confused and behave aggressively when reinforcers are removed.

## Time Away

Time away involves removing students from a task, situation, or materials until they are ready to come back and complete the task or correct the situation. For example, a student is throwing around math blocks instead of doing a math activity, so the teacher takes the blocks off the student's desk. The student has partial control, in that the teacher returns the blocks if the student asks for them and commits to doing the activity appropriately.

## Time Out

A student who is anxious or upset may need to leave the situation to calm down before any redirection or teaching of new behaviours can occur. Combine this approach with positive programming strategies such as teaching students to recognize when they are becoming anxious, and teaching them to independently remove themselves from situations before they lose control.

Because removal from the learning environment is a restrictive and serious form of intervention, use it only when less restrictive interventions have proved ineffective. Always use time out cautiously, carefully document the process that was followed, and follow board or district policies. Parents should be consulted during the development of the student's behaviour plan to gain their support of this strategy. Excessive use of time out can result in the student missing valuable instructional time and falling behind academically, which, in turn, can cause further behavioural issues as the child experiences frustration due to gaps in his or her learning.

Time out can be in the classroom or outside of it. If students stay in the room, the teacher removes them from an activity or group. They can continue to observe but not actually participate in the activity. Time out outside the room may involve directing students to a nearby hallway or a separate area. To ensure safety, monitor and supervise students throughout the time out.

Some students may purposely engage in negative behaviours to avoid group situations and structured tasks. Generally speaking, time-out consequences are only effective when students feel that they are missing out on positive experiences.

Clearly outline time-out procedures in the students' individualized education or program plans and/or individual behaviour support plans, and communicate the procedures to them, their parents, and administrators. Seek permission for using this procedure from administrators and parents prior to implementation. If, in collaboration with parents, it is decided that time-outs would be ineffective with a particular child, work together to determine alternative strategies for dealing with that child's inappropriate behaviour. Regular evaluation of the effectiveness of the procedure is critically important.

Never use consequences such as time out in isolation. Develop a comprehensive approach to behaviour management that is structured around positive behaviour supports to motivate students to display appropriate behaviours (see example of individual behaviour support plan on pages 76 to 78).

Time outs are for a minimal and predetermined time. When the time is over, the student returns to the situation, task, or activity. District guidelines provide guidance and parameters for the appropriate use of time outs.

For resources about using time out in schools, see our Web site: www.pearsoncanada.ca/ci

## Guidelines for Using Negative Consequences

- Make clear to students what the problem behaviour is and what the consequences are for engaging in that behaviour.
- Deliver the consequence. Do not just threaten to deliver the consequence.
- Recognize and embrace the use of negative consequences as a teaching tool, not a punishing tool. The consequence gives students another opportunity to learn that what they have done is problematic and that they can correct their behaviour.
- Be consistent. The severity of the consequence is not as important as its certainty. People speed because they get caught only sometimes. Students display problem behaviour because they sometimes get away with it. It is harder to learn to stop a behaviour if sometimes it is a problem and sometimes it is not.
- Be sensitive about when and how the consequence is delivered. If possible, avoid delivering a negative consequence in front of the student's peers.
- Deliver the negative consequences in a matter-of-fact way. When an adult shows emotion while delivering consequences, students tend to react emotionally and therefore don't think about what they should have done. They are less likely to learn from the consequence.
- Be aware of the relationship between memory, information processing, and consequences. For example, students with fetal alcohol spectrum disorder (FASD) have difficulty remembering or making associations between their behaviour and the consequences of their actions. Negative consequences may not motivate students with these types of disabilities to

reduce or eliminate the problem behaviour. The primary focus in these cases is to teach new or replacement behaviours and manage the environment to support positive behaviour.

## Avoid the Pitfalls of Punishment

Punishment is complex, and has many pitfalls.

- Punishment, which does not teach correct behaviour but rather temporarily eliminates problem behaviour, can be degrading and abusive. Students who are punished often develop a negative self-concept, especially if the punishment is arbitrary, inconsistent, or focused on the student's personality as opposed to the behaviour itself. These students may begin to see themselves as stupid, or believe they are unlikable and only capable of negative behaviour.
- If students have experienced a variety of negative emotional or physical punishments in their family and home life, they may feel the consequences delivered by the school are mild and/or irrelevant.
- The consequences a teacher gives in class may have less of an impact than potential consequences from other students. For example, Zenia acts out and does not participate in a class discussion. She would rather have peers see her as the class clown than as someone who doesn't know the answer and is "stupid" or "dumb."

Activities associated with punishment also tend to become punishing. For example:

- If a teacher corrects students frequently while they are reading, the students begin to feel that reading is a punishment.
- If a teacher requires a student who is weak in math to miss physical education class to do additional math questions, the student begins to feel that math is a punishment.
- If a teacher assigns a student an essay to reflect on a problem behaviour or incident, the student begins to feel that writing is punishing.
- Individual students may connect certain teachers, teacher assistants, or the principal with punishment if they see these people only when they receive a negative consequence.

# Collaborative Teamwork and a Wraparound Process

8

"Never doubt that a small group of thoughtful committed people can change the world. Indeed it is the only thing that ever has."

– Margaret Mead

Since students' problem behaviour pervades most areas of their home and school lives, a team approach is essential.

## A Team Approach

Students with behaviour disabilities need a team of professionals whose members work together to plan, implement, monitor, and evaluate programming, services, and supports. Generally, the classroom teacher, special education teacher, or guidance counsellor leads the team in developing goals and objectives that are educationally relevant.

Members of the team should include the classroom teacher, parents, the student (if age and developmentally appropriate), other school and jurisdiction staff who understand the student's needs, and other adults who frequently interact with the student. When required, the team may also include consultants, coaches, and facilitators with expertise in behavioural assessment and interventions. The team works collaboratively with other teachers, assistants, specialized teachers, behaviour specialists, and mental health professionals to meet the student's individual needs.

The team develops goals and objectives for the student at the beginning of each school year and links them to assessment results. They routinely monitor and evaluate the student's progress and make changes to the individualized education/program plan (IEP/IPP) accordingly throughout the academic year. Team members frequently communicate informally throughout the year in order to identify successful programming strategies and adjust the less successful ones.

## Knowledgeable and Skilled Staff

School staff who work with students with behaviour disabilities need to

- have knowledge about and experience with typically used and successful behavioural and cognitive strategies
- have ongoing access to learning opportunities, resources, and classroom support that could help them meet these students' behavioural needs
- be able to identify and implement positive behavioural interventions and then use data to evaluate the effectiveness of these interventions and make ongoing programming adjustments as required
- be knowledgeable about behaviours associated with particular disabilities such as AD/HD, autism, or FASD
- have the skills required to prevent problem behaviours and respond appropriately when acting-out behaviours occur

## Administrative Support

School administrators need to understand and actively support the teams that work with individual students with behaviour disabilities. Understanding the challenges the team is dealing with will help administrators make informed decisions about

- resource allocation
- application of school policies
- strategies to support staff capacity building

## Family Involvement

Students' achievement, attitudes, and behaviour all improve when parents and other family members are involved with the school. Working in partnership, the adults in a student's life can "wrap around" a student to develop effective programming, interventions, and supports.

Parents need to know specifically what behaviour is acceptable in the school and classroom. School staff need to work collaboratively with and talk to parents about strategies for dealing with inappropriate behaviours.

Have parents participate in the IEP/IPP development and review process. In addition to addressing academic and social needs, the individualized plans and day-to-day programming should recognize the student's unique cultural and family needs.

## Wraparound Process

The wraparound approach to services for students with behaviour disabilities involves a family-centred philosophy of care that links naturally with positive behaviour support systems. This team approach places the student and the significant adults in his or her life at the centre of the process. The adults involved are usually the parents but in some cases they include another relative or a friend or support person who has the legal right or parent or guardian's permission to participate.

The team members serve as resource people who can help school staff positively influence behaviours that compromise the student's safety and learning. The team members work together to set the student up for success. For example, if a student loves to work at a local garage and fix cars, the team may work with an employer to provide extra time working on cars as a reward for maintaining a good school attendance record.

Many students with intensive behavioural needs may be involved with a number of community agencies or service providers. The wraparound process encourages all services to work together intentionally and collaboratively.

## Onsite Community Partners

A team approach to providing a school-wide support system for students works best when it is onsite, multidisciplinary, and multi-level. Members of an onsite support team could include, but are not limited to

- school staff who work with the student
- board or district psychologist or counsellor
- public health staff
- dietitian
- social worker/mental health therapist
- attendance counsellor
- youth worker/family liaison worker
- community police resource officer

Having a community of caring adults located right in the school on a regularly scheduled basis (e.g., several hours each week or half-a-day a month) provides rich opportunities for

- building positive relationships
- teaching social skills and problem solving
- providing intervention and support on an as-needed basis

With these kinds of supports in place, students have more opportunities to gain the knowledge and skills to choose healthy behaviours, to make better life choices and, ultimately, to respond to life's changes and challenges with resiliency and emotional maturity.

This collaborative "all for one" approach—in which partners work together to support one school, one classroom, and one individual student, will help create a stable, caring environment for learning and teaching.

For more information about community partners and the "all for one" approach, see our Web site: www.pearsoncanada.ca/ci

# Data-Informed Decision-Making

9

"Find out what is working. Do more of it."

– Steve de Shazer,
Developer of solution focused brief therapy

Gathering and using data about a student's behaviour helps school staff to

- better understand the purpose and context of specific behaviours
- guide the development and implementation of behaviour support programming
- know when a behaviour is improving

Initially, collecting data about a student's problem behaviour provides valuable information about possible reasons for the behaviour. To collect this data, the school team systematically observes, records, and analyzes the student's behaviour across school settings.

Once staff have sufficient data on a student's behaviour, they are better prepared to make decisions about

- strategies for changing or replacing a problem behaviour
- developing an individual behaviour support plan
- evaluating and assessing the student's program and progress

## Data Collection Procedures[15]

Collect baseline data before beginning to teach new skills or develop plans for reinforcement and positive behaviour support. Use this data to compare students' performance at the outset with their performance at later dates.

Baseline data includes the frequency of a behaviour, the amount of time the behaviour is observed, and/or the level and intensity of the behaviour. Collect baseline data on typical behaviours for approximately three to five days, and on less frequent behaviours over a longer period.

15. The remainder of this chapter is adapted with permission from Karen Bain and Brenda Sautner, *BOATS: Behaviour, Observation, Assessment and Teaching Strategies*, 2nd ed. (Edmonton, AB: Special Education Council, The Alberta Teachers' Association, 2007), pp. 29–38.

The next stage of data collection is to observe and record the student's behaviour before and after positive behaviour support programming to show progress and monitor change.

## Tips for Collecting Data

- Observe problem behaviour often enough to accurately and clearly describe and document it in a variety of settings or contexts, at various times, and with different staff members. If a behaviour occurs constantly, observe and record the times during which the behaviour occurs, as well as the locations and surrounding conditions.
- Specify behaviours in observable and measurable terms that are easily recorded. Staff need to have a common understanding of what the behaviour looks like so that everyone knows when the behaviour occurs. Staff also need to know how to describe influential environmental conditions.
- The type, rigour, and method of data collection depends on the nature and severity of the problem and the kind of behaviour being observed.

Following is a suggested process for collecting data.

1. Select a problem behaviour that the student needs to modify or replace. Focus first on the most critical behavioural concerns.
2. Choose a data collection system that is effective and efficient, and one that is appropriate for the nature, extent, and/or frequency of the behaviour.
3. Collect the data.
4. Summarize and assess the data.
5. Use this analysis to
   - identify the function of the behaviour
   - determine desired behaviours and decide which ones take priority
   - select teaching strategies
   - develop an individual behaviour support plan

Specific methods of collecting data include event recording, interval recording, momentary time sampling, duration recording, and ABC recording (described on page 37).

## Event Recording

Count the number of times a discrete behaviour happens during an identified time period (e.g., class, day, or event). Count by making tally marks on the board, moving items from one pocket to another, or putting marks on a bracelet or tape on a wrist. This approach is not suitable for observing behaviours that occur at a very high rate because the counting process becomes too difficult.

*Example 1*

Each time a student shouts out during class, the teacher makes a mark on the board. This method may be suitable when the goal is to decrease call-outs and increase hand-raising.

| | | | |
|---|---|---|---|
| Math<br>~~||||~~ \|\| | Science<br>\|\|\| | Social<br>0 | Phys. Ed.<br>0 |
| Language Arts<br>\|\| | Home Room<br>0 | Lunch Room<br>0 | Library<br>\|\| |

*Example 2*

A student has a problem with swearing. The teacher keeps a chart like the one below and uses a checkmark to indicate each time this problem behaviour is observed.

Monday

| 1 | 2 | 3 | 4 | 5 | 6 | 7 | 8 | 9 | 10 | 11 | 12 | 13 | 14 | 15 |
|---|---|---|---|---|---|---|---|---|---|---|---|---|---|---|
| ✓ | ✓ | ✓ | ✓ | ✓ | ✓ | ✓ | ✓ | ✓ | ✓ | | | | | |

Tuesday

| 1 | 2 | 3 | 4 | 5 | 6 | 7 | 8 | 9 | 10 | 11 | 12 | 13 | 14 | 15 |
|---|---|---|---|---|---|---|---|---|---|---|---|---|---|---|
| ✓ | ✓ | ✓ | ✓ | ✓ | | | | | | | | | | |

This method simply counts the frequency of a problem behaviour. It does not provide any information about conditions, times, or situations.

## Interval Recording

Record behaviours as they occur within a set time. For example, divide a 10-minute assignment or task into 30-second intervals and note whether the behaviour occurs during each interval.

Or record behaviour that lasts throughout a whole interval. For example, divide a 30-minute period into 20-second intervals and record self-stimulatory behaviour when it occurs during the full 20 seconds.

To collect data using the interval recording method,

- define a specific time period for observation

- divide the observation period into equal intervals that are adequate for observing and recording behaviour reliably
- select a method of recording and note the materials required
- describe the behaviour to be observed in extremely clear terms so recording is consistent across observers

Try using a matrix that combines the time intervals with the student's daily timetable to determine behaviour patterns across settings or subject areas.

*Example*

A student often daydreams when math activities are assigned. He just sits, gazing at the ceiling fan and smiling. Indicate whether the behaviour occurs during a five-minute interval, using a checkmark for Yes and an X for No.

| | | | |
|---|---|---|---|
| 5 minutes ✓ | 10 minutes ✓ | 15 minutes ✓ | 20 minutes ✓ |
| 25 minutes ✗ | 30 minutes ✗ | 35 minutes ✗ | 40 minutes ✓ |

A timer or electronic signalling device such as an egg timer or counting clock can help the observer remember to record during each interval. Interval recording is best done by an objective observer who is not responsible for teaching at the same time, as it requires a high level of vigilance to be valid and reliable.

## Momentary Time Sampling

The observer sets up an interval of time and records whether the behaviour is occurring at the specific time the interval ends. This data collection method works for groups of students as well as individuals, and it allows an observer to record more than one behaviour at the same time.

*Example*

A buzzer rings at fixed/regular intervals (e.g., every 5 minutes) or at varying/random intervals (e.g., after 4 minutes, 7 minutes, and then 3 minutes). The teacher or observer scans the classroom and records behaviours at that precise time. The teacher may also praise students who are writing quietly during individual seatwork, record a mark by the names of students who are "on task," or use the buzzer ringing as a personal prompt to attend to individual students.

The following chart indicates whether individual students were "on task" at three selected times during a 20-minute creative writing session.

| Student's Name | Writing Interval 1 | Writing Interval 2 | Writing Interval 3 |
|---|---|---|---|
| Karen | ✓ | ✓ | ✓ |
| Hayley | ✗ | ✗ | ✓ |
| Myka | ✓ | ✓ | ✓ |
| Darci | ✗ | ✓ | ✓ |
| Lorraine | ✗ | ✗ | ✗ |

Momentary time sampling can be used effectively to improve the behaviour or performance of a group of students. Note that the measurement must take place several times in order to provide reliable and valid information.

## Duration Recording

Duration recording indicates the length of time a specific behaviour occurs. Recording starts at the time the individual begins the behaviour and stops when it ends. For example, the observer counts the number of minutes a student actively works at the computer, pays close attention during group discussions, or participates in a gym game or other social activity. Duration recording combined with event recording can be useful as well. For example, a teacher records how many times a student is out of his or her seat, and for how long each time (duration).

Duration recording requires a clock, wristwatch, stopwatch, or other timing device. Start timing each time the student begins the target behaviour, and stop timing when the behaviour ends. Duration recording is not a suitable data collection method if the behaviour does not have a clear beginning and end, or if the behaviour is frequent (unless someone other than the teacher does the recording).

*Example*

A student throws a tantrum when given work she dislikes. The observer starts the timer when the tantrum begins and stops it when it ends.

## Using Data Collection Systems

The following table summarizes the potential uses of recommended data collection systems.

| Behaviour | Event Recording | Interval Recording | Momentary Time Sampling | Duration Recording |
|---|---|---|---|---|
| Off task | | ✓ | | ✓ |
| Hitting others | ✓ | | | |
| Swearing | ✓ | | | |
| Yelling out | ✓ | ✓ | | |
| Spitting | ✓ | | | |
| Self-stimulation | ✓ | ✓ | | ✓ |
| Bothering others | | ✓ | | |
| Behaviour for which the function is unknown | ✓ | ✓ | ✓ | |

A data collection system provides baseline information that helps staff to clearly identify the nature, extent, and frequency of problem behaviours. Use data collection systems initially to make summary statements about the student's observed problem behaviours and set priorities for more comprehensive observations. Then use the results to develop hypotheses about situations; for example, whether certain reinforcements may be encouraging or maintaining a problem behaviour.

Continually collect behavioural data. Data collected before and after implementing a positive behaviour support plan helps staff to monitor whether the plan to change behaviour has been effective.

# Individual Behaviour Support Plans

10

> "... a behavioral support plan is a document that is designed to change the behavior of adults with the expectation that if adult behavior changes, the behavior of the student will change."
>
> – Robert Horner and George Sugai, "Developing Positive Behavioral Support Systems"

Students with behaviour disabilities may respond to some universal strategies used in the school-wide positive behaviour support system. However, these students require additional intensive and individualized strategies and support. These strategies need to be documented and communicated in a formal individual behaviour support plan based on these students' unique and individual characteristics. These step-by-step plans provide key information about a student's behaviour for staff who work with the student. The information in the plan needs to include

- key understandings about this student's behaviour
- conditions or antecedent events that are most likely to trigger the problem behaviour
- warning signs that the student is experiencing difficulty
- plans for diffusing the situation
- positive supports to help the student increase his or her abilities
- what peers need to learn to do to support this student
- other strategies school staff can use to support and encourage this student

TOOL

Tool 8 provides a sample template of an individual behaviour support plan.

Staff need to read this plan before they work with the student. The plan should be kept in the office, with duplicate copies with each teacher working with that student. Protocols must be in place to safeguard student records and to protect student confidentiality. The objective of the plan is that all staff working with the student are aware of and committed to using positive behaviour support strategies to create and maintain a safe learning environment for the student, other students, and school staff.

## Parent Involvement

It is important that staff collaborate with parents in the development of this plan so that parents support the proactive strategies and the preplanned consequences and crisis management plan.

### Sample Individual Behaviour Support Plan

**Re**: Sonny (13 years old, Grade 7)

**Objective of Plan**

Staff working with Sonny will be aware of and committed to using behaviour support procedures to maintain a safe environment for Sonny, other students, and staff.

Key understandings about Sonny ***(Functions of problem behaviour)***

- Academic pressures increase Sonny's anxiety—he sometimes gets physically aggressive to avoid certain academic tasks, especially in math.
- Sonny often feels that peers are teasing or rejecting him—he sometimes gets physically aggressive to avoid what he perceives as peer rejection.
- Sonny wants to have friends and be respected for his vast knowledge of video games and computers.

**Plan**

1. Staff working with Sonny and Sonny's parents/guardians will read and sign this plan.
2. Be aware of **antecedent events**. Problem behaviour is most likely to occur when
   - Sonny is presented with a new assignment, especially in math
   - Sonny thinks other students are making fun of him or rejecting him
   - Sonny misunderstands or overreacts to other students' casual comments
3. Be aware of **warning signs** that problem behaviour may escalate:
   - Sonny starts talking to himself.
   - Sonny approaches the student he believes is making fun of him or rejecting him.
   - Sonny reaches for a desk or another piece of furniture.
4. Immediate **plans to defuse** the situation:
   - Give Sonny a problem-solving card with calm-down choices (e.g., breathe deeply, go get a drink, don't react).

- If necessary, ask other students to quietly leave the area.
- Once Sonny has calmed down, he will outline a plan for upcoming activities, with assistance from a staff member.

5. **Positive behaviour supports** throughout the school year:
   - Before asking Sonny to carry out a new activity independently, give him the opportunity to successfully practise it in a group setting or with a peer.
   - To ensure success, give Sonny structured assignments (e.g., with completed sample, cue cards, reduced number of questions required), particularly in math and when longer writing assignments are required.
   - Work with Sonny each week to set personal goals re: completing assignments, getting along with peers. Review progress at the end of each week.
   - Select, teach, and practise problem-solving strategies. Record them on a cue card for easy reference.
   - Select, teach, and practise calm-down strategies. Record them on a cue card for easy reference.
   - Help Sonny to write a social story dealing with teasing (or perceived teasing).
   - Provide verbal praise privately when Sonny uses calm-down strategies.
   - Look for opportunities for Sonny to share the computer games and programs he creates with other students.
   - Send home weekly good news e-mails describing Sonny's recent successes.
6. Help **peers learn** to
   - understand that Sonny may not always understand their intentions
   - reduce joking and teasing that can be misinterpreted
   - include Sonny in their activities
7. Staff will provide **additional support** by
   - incorporating guided practice in calm-down strategies and problem solving for all students across the subject areas and throughout the school day
   - encouraging Sonny to join school computer club and providing informal coaching to help him create and maintain positive relationships with peers in this social setting

**Crisis Management Plan.** If aggressive or unsafe behaviour occurs in spite of proactive strategies, the school plan is as follows:

- Ask Sonny to leave the classroom and go to Ms. R's room. An adult walks with him.
- If he refuses to leave, hold up the red card and quietly ask the other students to pick up their materials and go to another area (e.g., the library).
- Have Sonny stay in Miss R's room until he calms down.

- Once he is calm, ask Sonny to express his feelings about the incident through drawing. With assistance, Sonny identifies another way of dealing with similar incidents in the future (by choosing one of his problem-solving strategies).
- Notify Sonny's parents of unsafe incidents. (Mom's cell number is 222–2222.)

I have read this plan and commit to using these supports when working with Sonny.

| Team members' signatures | Parents' signatures |
|---|---|
| ______________________ | ______________________ |
| ______________________ | ______________________ |
| Date | Review date |
| ______________________ | ______________________ |

Developing an individual behaviour support plan takes a team effort and should be done at the beginning of each school year or shortly after a student has been identified as needing a support plan.

## Key Understandings

Begin the planning process by identifying at least three key behaviours that significantly impact this student's school success. Use data from the functional behavioural assessment to describe typical problem behaviours and the typical functions of these behaviours. In addition, identify at least one positive or strength-based behaviour. These behaviours will be the focus of the plan.

Consider the types of problem behaviours that might be targeted from the following lists.

### Internalizing Behaviours

- Anxiety
  - worries incessantly
  - is fearful
  - is nervous
  - avoids tasks or situations

- Depression
  - – cries easily
  - – is pessimistic
  - – is easily upset
- Somatization (illness related to psychological distress)
  - – has headaches and/or stomach aches
  - – complains of general pain or fatigue
- Withdrawal
  - – refuses to talk or join in group activities
  - – avoids others
- Inattention
  - – has a short attention span
  - – does not complete tasks
  - – is easily distracted

## Externalizing Behaviours

- Anger control
  - – has temper outbursts or "explosions"
  - – is unable to regulate emotions
- Aggression
  - – teases others
  - – breaks others' things
  - – threatens others
  - – physically hurts others
  - – swears at or is rude to others
- Hyperactivity/impulsivity
  - – is excitable
  - – interrupts others
  - – is restless or overactive
  - – cannot wait to take turns
  - – talks excessively
- Oppositional behaviour
  - – argues
  - – disrupts the play of others
  - – annoys others on purpose
  - – refuses to follow directions or respond to requests
  - – breaks rules, including those against lying and stealing

The list above does not identify the reasons for specific behaviours. For example, a student may not be completing tasks for a variety of reasons, including inattention, oppositional behaviour, or anxiety. To identify functions of these behaviours, use data gathered from a functional behavioural assessment (FBA). (For more information on FBA, see pages 35 to 41.)

### Determine Priorities

Students with behaviour disabilities often display several challenging behaviours, and many of them urgently need to be addressed. If a behaviour support plan attempts to address too many challenging behaviours at once, the plan becomes too complex and unwieldy, and it ultimately fails. Even when only one or two behaviours are targeted for change in the individualized education or program plan (IEP/IPP) and behaviour support plan, school staff continue to address the other behaviours through regular rules and routines.

Begin by choosing **one** behaviour of concern as the target for intervention in the behaviour support plan. This choice often depends on factors such as the impact of that behaviour on the student's

- well-being and the well-being of others (Behaviours that place the student at risk or other staff or students at risk must be addressed first.)
- participation and learning
- relationships with other students and teachers
- ability to learn in the classroom

Another factor to consider in choosing the target behaviour is the likelihood of success over the short term; for example, within three months. Once students have had success in one area, they can build on that success and systematically address other problem behaviours. Parents can often participate in the identification of priority behaviours.

### Identify Function of Behaviour

When priority behaviours have been identified, use data from a functional behavioural analysis to determine the function or purpose of each type of problem behaviour. Include a description of the function in the "Key understandings" section of the plan.

## Antecedents, Warning Signs, and Plans for Defusing

Use data gathered about this student's behaviour to identify antecedents or contexts in which the problem behaviour is most likely to occur. This will give staff working with the student a better idea of how they might structure situations to prevent problem behaviour and encourage positive behaviour.

Identifying warning signs that the student is beginning to experience difficulty can help staff be aware of what to look for in the classroom in order to defuse potentially problematic situations. Having a plan in place to defuse situations will give staff confidence to act proactively and will help students better understand their role in managing their own behaviour.

## Positive Supports

Identifying positive supports for a student is the most important part of an individual behaviour support plan. Identifying proactive strategies that staff can use to help the student develop and maintain positive behaviours to replace problem behaviours is key.

This section of the plan also identifies specific skills and concepts that need to be taught, practised, and reinforced, and the specific types of reinforcers that are effective for this student. These supports should be in place across school environments and throughout the school year.

## Role of Peers

The choice of a target problem behaviour in the plan is also determined by the impact the behaviour is having on other students.

Consider whether the behaviour is affecting their

- ability to learn
- participation in the class
- stress level in class (e.g., feeling of safety)
- tendency to imitate the negative behaviour

In inclusive settings, staff must find ways to implement plans that do not stigmatize students with behaviour disabilities but also do not disrupt the learning or compromise the safety or well-being of other students.

Peers can support positive behaviour when they understand what they can do to help. Classroom behaviour expectations that support inclusive and supportive behaviour (such as including others or not engaging in teasing or bullying) can also create a supportive structure in which peers model positive behaviour and effective social skills.

## Additional Support

This part of the plan identifies other opportunities staff can use to model, teach, and support positive behaviour throughout the school day. Many of these proactive strategies will benefit all students, not only students with behaviour disabilities.

## Crisis Management Plan

Although the goal is to prevent a crisis from ever occurring, recognize that some students with behaviour disabilities may occasionally become very agitated. In such cases, the behaviour support plan for that individual student becomes a crisis management tool. All staff working with the student, and perhaps other students in the class, need to be aware of and understand this crisis management plan, which ideally has been developed by the whole planning team, including parents.

The main focus of the plan is identifying steps for decreasing the likelihood that the problem behaviour will occur, but there needs to be a plan in place in the event that the interventions are not effective.

If a behaviour escalates and requires this alternative plan, the team needs to revisit the behaviour support plan as soon as possible to adjust the level and type of individualized intervention.

### Physical Intervention

Physical intervention is a crisis management technique, not a strategy for managing behaviour. Physical interventions are not designed to reduce the frequency or severity of negative behaviours but rather to ensure the students' safety. Consequently, these interventions are used only in emergencies. Teachers need to consult with administrators to determine which interventions are approved for use in their jurisdiction, what training is available, and what documentation, including communication with parents, is required. Only staff who have received specific training should attempt physical interventions. The goal should always be to increase and improve proactive behaviour interventions so physical intervention is never necessary.

### Crisis Management Protocols

For more information on threat assessment protocols, refer to our Web site: www.pearsoncanada.ca/ci

Many jurisdictions have developed risk threat assessment protocols that assist school personnel in identifying students who may have suicidal or homicidal intentions. One of the goals of a threat assessment protocol is that adults react appropriately—neither overreact or underreact—to problem behaviours.

Protocols generally involve a multidisciplinary team using a set of guiding questions to assess the risk a student poses.

The crisis management plan section in a student's individual behaviour support plan would align with the jurisdiction protocol developed for all students. However, depending on the specific terms of the jurisdiction protocol, and the developmental needs of the individual student with behaviour disabilities, the intervention most appropriate and effective with that student might be slightly different.

## Individualized Education or Program Plans

An individualized education or program plan (IEP/IPP) for a student with behaviour disabilities should include three to five goals related to behaviours that interfere with or present a barrier to the student's learning or the learning of other students. The individual behaviour support plan outlines ways to act on and support the behaviour goals identified in the IEP/IPP.

These plans generally contain

- assessment data (diagnostic assessment data used to determine special education programming and services)
- current level of performance and achievement
- strengths and areas of need
- measurable goals and objectives
- procedures for evaluating student progress
- identification of coordinated support services
- relevant medical information
- required classroom accommodations
- transition plans
- information about formal review of progress at regularly scheduled reporting periods
- year-end summary
- parents' signatures to indicate agreement with the plan

For more information about individualized education or program plans, see our Web site: www.pearsoncanada.ca/ci

Essential to the success of the plan is engaging parents/guardians and, whenever possible, the students in its development and monitoring of its progress.

TOOL

# Sample Tools

1. Tips for Parents: Participating in Behaviour Support Planning
2. Solution-Focused Meetings
3. Home–School Communication Book
4. Environmental Classroom Scan
5. Behaviour Observation and Data Collection Chart
6. Problem Behaviour Questionnaire
7. Functional Behavioural Assessment Plan
8. Individual Behaviour Support Plan

TOOL 1

# Tips for Parents: Participating in Behaviour Support Planning

Behaviour support planning is the process by which families, teachers, and other school staff work as a team to meet the individual needs of students with behaviour disabilities. As a parent, you are an important member of your child's school team.

You can participate in the behaviour support planning process by

- providing information about your child's past experience and his or her goals, interests, and areas of need
- regularly contacting your child's teachers
- taking an active role in the decisions made for your child
- learning about available services and resources
- working with your child at home to support the goals set through the behaviour support planning process
- actively participating in behaviour support planning meetings

## Before Behaviour Support Planning Meetings

- Discuss the positive elements in the behaviour support plan with your child.
- Find out about your child's involvement and role in the meeting. Decide if your child will benefit from participating in the meeting, or at least part of the meeting.
- Review the comments from your child's last report card, and goals and objectives from the last behaviour support plan. What progress have you seen? Note areas of concern.
- Ask your child questions or, if your child attends the meeting, he or she may be able to give input directly. For example:
  - What do you like best about school? What do you feel are your successes?
  - What problems do we need to find solutions for? What changes would help you learn better at school?
  - What would you like to happen this year?

*Class Interrupted: Strategies for Positive Behaviour (Individual Focus)*
The right to reproduce this page is restricted to purchasing schools.
Copyright © 2010 Pearson Canada Inc.

## Tips for Parents: Participating in Behaviour Support Planning (continued)

- Be prepared. Jot down questions and concerns that you want to discuss. For example:
  - Whom should I call if I have concerns about my child's school program?
  - Will the team review the behaviour support plan every term?
  - What kinds of changes in our home does the school need to know about?
- Prioritize your concerns.

## At Behaviour Support Planning Meetings

- Ask about new assessments, reports, or observations.
- Ask about your child's strengths, interests, areas of growth, areas of need, and friendships.
- Ask any other questions you have about your child's progress or programming.
- Talk about your present and future goals for your child.
- Discuss your specific concerns about your child.
- Talk about home conditions that may affect your child's performance or behaviour at school and provide recent documents or medical updates.
- Circulate samples of work your child has completed at home, if you think this can help other team members understand your child better. Ask to see samples of work your child has done at school.

## At the Close of Behaviour Support Planning Meetings

- Establish mutually agreed-upon goals and strategies for your child.
- Find out how you can support your child at home.
- Take notes on timelines, recommendations; for example, suggestions for additional services or assessments.
- Verbally summarize your understanding and interpretation of the decisions made, actions team members will take, timelines, and roles and responsibilities of each participant.



*Class Interrupted: Strategies for Positive Behaviour (Individual Focus)*
The right to reproduce this page is restricted to purchasing schools.
Copyright © 2010 Pearson Canada Inc.

Tips for Parents: Participating in Behaviour Support Planning (continued)

- Give feedback to the people working with your child about areas where you have noted positive effort, growth, or change.
- Sign the behaviour support plan to indicate your agreement. If you do not agree with the behaviour support plan and do not wish to sign, the school has an obligation to document the reasons for your decision and the actions taken to resolve the issue.
- Ask for a copy of the behaviour support plan to refer to at home.
- Decide on the next meeting date.

## After Behaviour Support Planning Meetings

- Give your child feedback from the meeting.
- Discuss what needs to happen in order to reach the goals of the behaviour support plan. Discuss your child's role and how school staff and your family will support the plan.

## To Review the Effectiveness of Your Child's Behaviour Support Plan, Ask Yourself These Questions

- How does the behaviour support plan build on my child's strengths?
- How does the behaviour support plan address my child's individual needs?
- Does the behaviour support plan focus on key goals for my child?
- How are supports tailored to my child's strengths, areas of need, and learning preferences?
- Does the behaviour support plan use more than one source of assessment data to determine strengths and areas of need?
- If several teachers are responsible for my child's education program, do all of them have access to the behaviour support plan so they can use it to plan instruction, monitor progress, and help measure success?
- Is the school frequently monitoring progress toward the goals of the behaviour support plan? If my child is not demonstrating progress, does the team review the program and make changes?

*Class Interrupted: Strategies for Positive Behaviour (Individual Focus)*
The right to reproduce this page is restricted to purchasing schools.
Copyright © 2010 Pearson Canada Inc.

TOOL 2

# Solution-Focused Meetings

Solution-focused meetings can effectively resolve particularly difficult situations or promote communication among all members of the school team. When everyone provides open, honest, and respectful input, the teaching staff, parents, and the student will be more committed to the behaviour planning process.

Following is an example of a process to use in a solution-focused meeting.

1. One member of the team agrees to act as the facilitator. This individual needs to be positive, attentive, task-oriented, and have the ability to clarify issues and summarize collaborative decisions. The facilitator must help each team member stay on topic and work toward appropriate, practical solutions.

2. The facilitator begins the meeting by inviting the person who initiated the meeting to state his or her concern clearly and concisely. Find out specifically what this person wants to happen as a result of this meeting.

3. The team members ask questions to clear up uncertainties about what the issue is or what the circumstances are. The facilitator may need to encourage team members to look for factors that appear to trigger or contribute to the problem, and to identify and analyze conditions that seem to alleviate the problem. As part of this analysis, team members may also identify the student's strengths and available resources.

4. Once the problem or issue is clearly defined, the team uses a round-table brainstorming session to suggest ways to solve the problem. All ideas are recorded on chart paper. At this stage let ideas flow freely and do not comment directly on any one idea.

5. The facilitator and the referring teacher review the strategies together and then rate each suggestion by assigning a number value.

   For example:

   1 = an idea or strategy that the teacher and/or parent wants to try

   2 = an idea or strategy that has merit, but is not a priority

   3 = an idea or strategy that has already been tried and didn't seem to resolve the issue

   4 = an idea or strategy that is not immediately practical at this time



Class Interrupted: Strategies for Positive Behaviour (Individual Focus)
The right to reproduce this page is restricted to purchasing schools.
Copyright © 2010 Pearson Canada Inc.

6. The team develops an action plan for each strategy selected, including materials and resources required, persons responsible, and dates for follow-up and review.
7. The facilitator closes the meeting by thanking everyone and asking for feedback on the process. The team generally agrees to meet for a progress review in four to six weeks.

A sample planner for a solution-focused meeting follows on the next page.

---

Adapted from "Problem Solving Teams: A Thirty-Minute Peer-Helping Model," in Gordon L. Porter and Diane Richler (eds.), *Changing Canadian Schools: Perspectives on Disability and Inclusion* (North York, ON: The Roeher Institute, 1991), pp. 224–228. Reproduced with permission from the Canadian Association of Community Living.

*Class Interrupted: Strategies for Positive Behaviour (Individual Focus)*
The right to reproduce this page is restricted to purchasing schools.
Copyright © 2010 Pearson Canada Inc.

TOOL 2

# Sample Planner for a Solution-Focused Meeting

Date ______________________________

Referring member of the school team ______________________________

Team members participating in the meeting

______________________ ______________________

______________________ ______________________

______________________ ______________________

Student's name ______________________________

A. Key concern

______________________________

______________________________

B. What we would like to see happen/change

______________________________

______________________________

C. Description of student's strengths and priority areas of need

| Strengths | Areas of need | Other resources |
|---|---|---|
| | | |

D. Potential strategies — What can make this happen?

- ______________________ ______________________
- ______________________ ______________________

E. Timelines ______________________________

F. Responsibility ______________________________

G. Follow-up meeting date ______________________________



Class Interrupted: Strategies for Positive Behaviour (Individual Focus)
The right to reproduce this page is restricted to purchasing schools.
Copyright © 2010 Pearson Canada Inc.

# Home–School Communication Book

TOOL 3

## My School Day

Date ____________________

| | Polite voice | | Hands and feet to myself | | Following teacher's requests | |
|---|---|---|---|---|---|---|
| | Me | My teacher | Me | My teacher | Me | My teacher |
| Language Arts<br>9:00 to 10:30 | | | | | | |
| Math<br>10:45 to 12:00 | | | | | | |
| Science<br>Phys Ed<br>1:00 to 2:15 | | | | | | |
| Social Studies<br>Wrap-up<br>2:30 to 3:30 | | | | | | |

4–*great!* 3–*okay* 2–*needs work* 1–*not acceptable*

What went well today

____________________

____________________

Teacher's signature ____________________

What we need to work on

____________________

____________________

Encouraging words from parents

____________________

*Class Interrupted: Strategies for Positive Behaviour (Individual Focus)*
The right to reproduce this page is restricted to purchasing schools.
Copyright © 2010 Pearson Canada Inc.

TOOL 4

# Environmental Classroom Scan

Use the following questions to assess how the classroom's physical set-up accommodates the needs of students, particularly students with behaviour disabilities.

### Storage of Outside Clothing

- Is there adequate and clearly labelled storage for students' outside clothes, backpacks, and lunch bags?
- Is there adequate space for students to remove or put on outer clothes without crowding?
- Is the coat area easy to supervise and located close to the teaching area?

### Student Desks

- Does the desk arrangement allow all students to
  - see the teaching area
  - participate in class discussion
  - have adequate space to work independently?
- Are there particular seating spots that accommodate students with major attention difficulties?
- Are student desks the appropriate size and in good repair?

### Storage of Equipment and Materials

- Is there a designated area where students can put their homework books at the beginning of the school day?
- Is there adequate storage for students' personal school supplies?
- Is shelving organized and clutter-free?
- Are storage areas labelled so students can find and return materials independently?
- Is there an area for storing materials and equipment out of sight?
- Are books displayed so students can see the covers and are encouraged to read?



Class Interrupted: Strategies for Positive Behaviour (Individual Focus)
The right to reproduce this page is restricted to purchasing schools.
Copyright © 2010 Pearson Canada Inc.

## Environmental Classroom Scan (continued)

### Work Areas

- Are areas in the classroom clearly defined?
- Is a private, secluded space available where students can go to work quietly by themselves or use as a safe place to calm down?

### Physical Set-up of the Classroom

- Do the colours of the room create a calming, harmonious environment?
- Does the furniture arrangement allow for good traffic flow?
- Are the major traffic areas located away from the main work area?
- Do wall displays contribute to a sense of order?
- Are nonessential decorations kept to a minimum?
- Are all areas of the classroom visible to the teacher to permit monitoring and supervision throughout the day?

### Sound

- Do the acoustics allow teachers and students to clearly and easily hear one another when speaking at normal conversational volume?
- Are carpeting or chair leg protectors used to muffle the noise of moving chairs and desks?
- Are there clear classroom expectations about talking during activities?
- Is music used to cue transitions and provide a calming background to enhance students' ability to focus on specific tasks?
- Are sounds from the hallway and windows sufficiently muffled?
- Is the school-wide messaging system used at set times during the day so teachers can encourage students to focus on listening?
- Is the sound quality of the intercom clear and at an appropriate volume?
- Is there minimal sound from lights and the heating system?

*Class Interrupted: Strategies for Positive Behaviour (Individual Focus)*
The right to reproduce this page is restricted to purchasing schools.
Copyright © 2010 Pearson Canada Inc.

## Environmental Classroom Scan (continued)

**Lighting**

- Are lights in good repair, with minimal humming and flickering?
- Is the lighting adequate for a range of learning activities?

**Visual Cues**

- Are signs and pictures at the students' eye level?
- Is an easy-to-read daily schedule clearly visible?
- Are classroom rules written in positive language and posted for easy reference?
- Are classroom supplies and equipment clearly labelled to establish ownership and facilitate retrieval and storage?
- Are only essential visuals posted?
- Are the visual cues in the classroom student-friendly and consistent with learning?



*Class Interrupted: Strategies for Positive Behaviour (Individual Focus)*
The right to reproduce this page is restricted to purchasing schools.
Copyright © 2010 Pearson Canada Inc.

TOOL 5

# Behaviour Observation and Data Collection Chart

When determining the function of inappropriate target behaviours in order to plan behaviour change interventions, observe the behaviour and collect information. Document the behaviour as factually as possible. Rather than speculating on the function of behaviour in the absence of good data, gather facts that are observable and measurable.

A = **Antecedent:** events in the environment that occur immediately before the target behaviour

B = **Behaviour:** actual behaviour, described in specific terms (including duration and intensity)

C = **Consequence:** events in the environment that occur directly after the behaviour

## ABC Chart

Name of student ______________________________

Target behaviour ____________________ Date ____________

| Time, Setting, Social Situation | Antecedent Event(s) | Behaviour Description | Consequence Event(s) |
|---|---|---|---|
| | | | |


The right to reproduce this page is restricted to purchasing schools.
Copyright © 2010 Pearson Canada Inc.

TOOL 6

# Problem Behaviour Questionnaire

Student ______________________ School ______________________

Teacher ______________________ Grade ________ Date ________

Specific behaviour description

______________________________________________

______________________________________________

Directions: Consider a typical episode of the problem behaviour described above and circle the frequency at which each of the following statements is true.

| | Never | 10% | 25% | 50% | 75% | 90% | Always |
|---|---|---|---|---|---|---|---|
| 1. Does the problem behaviour occur and persist when you make a request to perform a task? | 0 | 1 | 2 | 3 | 4 | 5 | 6 |
| 2. When the problem behaviour occurs, do you redirect the student to get back to task or follow rules? | 0 | 1 | 2 | 3 | 4 | 5 | 6 |
| 3. During a conflict with peers, if the student engages in the problem behaviour, do peers leave the student alone? | 0 | 1 | 2 | 3 | 4 | 5 | 6 |
| 4. When the problem behaviour occurs, do peers verbally respond to or laugh at the student? | 0 | 1 | 2 | 3 | 4 | 5 | 6 |
| 5. Is the problem behaviour more likely to occur following a conflict outside the classroom (e.g., bus write up)? | 0 | 1 | 2 | 3 | 4 | 5 | 6 |
| 6. Does the problem behaviour occur to get your attention when you are working with other students? | 0 | 1 | 2 | 3 | 4 | 5 | 6 |
| 7. Does the problem behaviour occur in the presence of specific peers? | 0 | 1 | 2 | 3 | 4 | 5 | 6 |
| 8. Is the problem behaviour more likely to continue to occur throughout the day following an earlier episode? | 0 | 1 | 2 | 3 | 4 | 5 | 6 |

*Diagnostique* 19, 2–3. Copyright 1994 by Sage Publications Inc. Journals. Reproduced with permission of Sage Publications Inc. Journals in the format of Textbook via Copyright Clearance Center.



*Class Interrupted: Strategies for Positive Behaviour (Individual Focus)*
The right to reproduce this page is restricted to purchasing schools.
Copyright © 2010 Pearson Canada Inc.

| | Never | 10% | 25% | 50% | 75% | 90% | Always |
|---|---|---|---|---|---|---|---|
| 9. Does the problem behaviour occur during specific academic activities? | 0 | 1 | 2 | 3 | 4 | 5 | 6 |
| 10. Does the problem behaviour stop when peers stop interacting with the student? | 0 | 1 | 2 | 3 | 4 | 5 | 6 |
| 11. Does the problem behaviour occur when peers are attending to other students? | 0 | 1 | 2 | 3 | 4 | 5 | 6 |
| 12. If the student engages in the problem behaviour, do you provide one-to-one instruction to get the student back on task? | 0 | 1 | 2 | 3 | 4 | 5 | 6 |
| 13. Will the student stop doing the problem behaviour if you stop making requests or end an activity? | 0 | 1 | 2 | 3 | 4 | 5 | 6 |
| 14. If the student engages in the problem behaviour, do peers stop interacting with the student? | 0 | 1 | 2 | 3 | 4 | 5 | 6 |
| 15. Is the problem behaviour more likely to occur following unscheduled events or disruptions in classroom routines? | 0 | 1 | 2 | 3 | 4 | 5 | 6 |

Circle the score given for each question from the scale below the corresponding question number (**in bold**).

| Payoff | Peers | | | | | | Adults | | | | | | Setting Events | | |
|---|---|---|---|---|---|---|---|---|---|---|---|---|---|---|---|
| | Escape | | | Attention | | | Escape | | | Attention | | | | | |
| | **3** | **10** | **14** | **4** | 7 | **11** | **1** | **9** | **13** | **2** | **6** | **12** | **5** | **8** | **15** |
| Always | 6 | 6 | 6 | 6 | 6 | 6 | 6 | 6 | 6 | 6 | 6 | 6 | 6 | 6 | 6 |
| 90% | 5 | 5 | 5 | 5 | 5 | 5 | 5 | 5 | 5 | 5 | 5 | 5 | 5 | 5 | 5 |
| 75% | 4 | 4 | 4 | 4 | 4 | 4 | 4 | 4 | 4 | 4 | 4 | 4 | 4 | 4 | 4 |
| 50% | 3 | 3 | 3 | 3 | 3 | 3 | 3 | 3 | 3 | 3 | 3 | 3 | 3 | 3 | 3 |
| 25% | 2 | 2 | 2 | 2 | 2 | 2 | 2 | 2 | 2 | 2 | 2 | 2 | 2 | 2 | 2 |
| 10% | 1 | 1 | 1 | 1 | 1 | 1 | 1 | 1 | 1 | 1 | 1 | 1 | 1 | 1 | 1 |
| Never | 0 | 0 | 0 | 0 | 0 | 0 | 0 | 0 | 0 | 0 | 0 | 0 | 0 | 0 | 0 |
| | Total _____ of 18 | | | Total _____ of 18 | | | Total _____ of 18 | | | Total _____ of 18 | | | Total _____ of 18 | | |

*Class Interrupted: Strategies for Positive Behaviour (Individual Focus)*
The right to reproduce this page is restricted to purchasing schools.
Copyright © 2010 Pearson Canada Inc.

TOOL 7

# Functional Behavioural Assessment Plan

Student ______________________ Teacher ______________

Class/Grade ____________________ Date ______________

| Questions | Outcomes/Action |
|---|---|
| 1. Describe the **problem** behaviour. What does it look like (description)?<br>– observable and measurable terms<br>– frequency and/or duration | |
| 2. Under what general conditions do **problem** behaviours tend to occur? Where? When? | |
| 3. Under what general conditions do **problem** behaviours tend not to occur? | |
| 4. What types of events or stimuli *immediately* precede **problem** behaviour? | |
| 5. What types of consequences typically follow instances of **problem** behavour? | |
| 6. What types of consequences typically follow instances of desired behaviour? | |
| 7. What is a testable explanation (hypothesis) of the behaviour? What is the main function of the behaviour? Why does the **problem** behaviour occur? | |
| 8. What do you want the student to do instead? Will it serve the same function? | |
| 9. Does your data support the hypothesized function of the behaviour? | |
| 10. What is the primary function of the behaviour? | |

(Scott and Nelson, 1999)



*Class Interrupted: Strategies for Positive Behaviour (Individual Focus)*
The right to reproduce this page is restricted to purchasing schools.
Copyright © 2010 Pearson Canada Inc.

# Individual Behaviour Support Plan

TOOL 8

**Re:** ______________________________________________

## Objective of plan

Staff working with ____________________ will be aware of and committed to using behaviour support procedures to maintain a safe learning environment for ____________________, other students, and staff.

Key understandings about ______________________________
***(Functions of problem behaviour)***

______________________________________________

______________________________________________

______________________________________________

______________________________________________

## Plan

1. Staff working with ____________________ will read and sign this plan.
2. Be aware of **antecedent events**. Problem behaviour is most likely to occur when

   ______________________________________________

   ______________________________________________

   ______________________________________________

   ______________________________________________

3. Be aware of **warning signs** that problem behaviour may escalate.

   ______________________________________________

   ______________________________________________

   ______________________________________________

   ______________________________________________


The right to reproduce this page is restricted to purchasing schools.
Copyright © 2010 Pearson Canada Inc.

## Individual Behaviour Support Plan (continued)

4. Immediate **plans to defuse** the situation

- ____________________________________
- ____________________________________
- ____________________________________
- ____________________________________
- ____________________________________
- ____________________________________

5. **Positive behaviour supports** throughout the school year

- ____________________________________
- ____________________________________
- ____________________________________
- ____________________________________
- ____________________________________
- ____________________________________

6. Help **peers learn** to

- ____________________________________
- ____________________________________
- ____________________________________
- ____________________________________
- ____________________________________
- ____________________________________



*Class Interrupted: Strategies for Positive Behaviour (Individual Focus)*
The right to reproduce this page is restricted to purchasing schools.
Copyright © 2010 Pearson Canada Inc.

## Individual Behaviour Support Plan (continued)

7. Staff will provide **additional support** by

- ______________________________
- ______________________________
- ______________________________
- ______________________________
- ______________________________
- ______________________________

**Crisis Management Plan.** If aggressive or unsafe behaviour occurs in spite of proactive strategies, the school has a plan, with steps to take and staff responses for each level of escalation.

- ______________________________
- ______________________________
- ______________________________
- ______________________________

I have read this plan and commit to using these supports when working with ____________________.

| Team members' signatures | Parents' signatures |
| --- | --- |
| ______________________ | ______________________ |
| ______________________ | ______________________ |

| Date | Review date |
| --- | --- |
| ______________________ | ______________________ |
| ______________________ | ______________________ |

*Class Interrupted: Strategies for Positive Behaviour (Individual Focus)*
The right to reproduce this page is restricted to purchasing schools.
Copyright © 2010 Pearson Canada Inc.

# References

Alberta Education. *Essential Components of Educational Programming for Students with Autism Spectrum Disorders.* Edmonton, AB: Alberta Education, 2006.

Alberta Education. *Essential Components of Educational Programming for Students with Behaviour Disabilities.* Edmonton, AB: Alberta Education, 2006.

Alberta Education. *Focusing on Success: Teaching Students with Attention Deficit/Hyperactivity Disorder.* Edmonton, AB: Alberta Education, 2006.

Alberta Learning. *Guidelines for Using Timeout in Schools.* Edmonton, AB: Alberta Learning, 2002.

Alberta Education. *Individualized Program Planning.* Edmonton, AB: Alberta Education, 2005.

Alberta Learning. *The Learning Team: A Handbook for Parents of Children with Special Needs.* Edmonton, AB: Alberta Learning, 2003.

Alberta Learning. *Teaching Students with Autism Spectrum Disorders.* Book 9 in the Programming for Students with Special Needs series. Edmonton, AB: Alberta Learning, 2003.

Alberta Learning. *Teaching Students with Emotional Disorders and/or Mental Illnesses.* Book 8 in the Programming for Students with Special Needs series. Edmonton, AB: Alberta Learning, 2000.

Alberta Learning. *Teaching Students with Fetal Alcohol Spectrum Disorder.* Book 10 in the Programming for Students with Special Needs series. Edmonton, AB: Alberta Learning, 2004.

Bailey, Becky. *7 Skills Poster Set.* Oviedo, FL: Loving Guidance, 2003.

Bain, Karen, and Brenda Sautner. *BOATS: Behaviour, Observation, Assessment and Teaching Strategies.* 2nd ed. Edmonton, AB: Special Education Council, The Alberta Teachers' Association, 2007.

Barkley, Russell A., and Christine M. Benton. *Your Defiant Child: 8 Steps to Better Behavior.* New York, NY: The Guilford Press, 1998.

Bellanca, James. "Teaching for Intelligence: In Search of Best Practices." *Phi Delta Kappan* 79, 9 (1998), pp. 658–660.

Belvel, Patricia Sequeira, and Maya Marcia Jordan. *Rethinking Classroom Management: Strategies for Prevention, Intervention, and Problem Solving.* Thousand Oaks, CA: Corwin Press, Inc., 2003.

Beran, Tanya B. "A Closer Look at the Relationship Between Bullying and Behaviour Problems: A Syndrome of Misconduct." *Exceptionality Education Canada* 15, 3 (2005), pp. 42–55.

Boynton, Mark, and Christine Boynton. *The Educator's Guide to Preventing and Solving Discipline Problems.* Alexandria, VA: Association for Supervision and Curriculum Development, 2005.

Chafouleas, Sandra, T. Chris Riley-Tillman, and George Sugai. *School-Based Behavioral Assessment: Informing Intervention and Instruction.* The Guilford Practical Intervention in the Schools series. New York, NY: Guilford Press, 2007.

Colvin, Geoff. *Managing the Cycle of Acting-out Behavior in the Classroom.* 2nd ed. Eugene, OR: Behavior Associates, 2004.

Colvin, Geoff, Edward J. Kame'enui, and George Sugai. "School-wide and Classroom Management: Reconceptualizing the Integration and Management of Students with Behavior Problems in General Education." *Education and Treatment of Children* 16, 4 (1993), pp. 361–381.

Curwin, Richard, Allen Mendler, and Brian Mendler. *Discipline with Dignity.* Alexandria, VA: Association for Supervision and Curriculum Development, 2008.

Eber, Lucille, and C. Michael Nelson. "School-Based Wraparound Planning: Integrating Services for Students with Emotional and Behavioral Needs." *American Journal of Orthopsychiatry* 67, 3 (1997), pp. 385–395.

Gottfredson, Denise C., Gary D. Gottfredson, and Stacy Skroban. "A Multimodel School-Based Prevention Demonstration." *Journal of Adolescent Research* 11, 1 (1996), pp. 97–115.

Greene, Ross W. *The Explosive Child: A New Approach for Understanding and Parenting Easily Frustrated, Chronically Inflexible Children.* Revised and updated ed. New York, NY: HarperCollins Publishers, 2005.

Gresham, Frank M. "Current Status and Future Directions of School-Based Behavioural Interventions." *School Psychology Review* 33 (2004), pp. 326–343.

Hieneman, Meme, Glen Dunlap, and Donald Kincaid. "Positive Support Strategies for Students with Behavioral Disorders in General Education Settings." *Psychology in the Schools* 42, 8 (2005), pp. 779–794.

Horner, Robert H., and George Sugai. "Developing Positive Behavioral Support Systems." In George Sugai and Timothy J. Lewis, *Developing Positive Behavioral Support for Students with Challenging Behaviors* (Reston, VA: Council for Children with Behavioral Disorders, a division of The Council for Exceptional Children, 1999), pp. 15–23.

Horner, Robert H., George Sugai, Anne W. Todd, and Teri Lewis-Palmer. "Elements of Behavior Support Plans: A Technical Brief." *Exceptionality* 8, 3 (1999–2000), pp. 205–215.

Kurcinka, Mary Sheedy. *Raising Your Spirited Child: A Guide for Parents Whose Child Is More Intense, Sensitive, Perceptive, Persistent, Energetic.* New York, NY: HarperCollins, 1991.

Lewis, Timothy J., Terrance M. Scott, and George Sugai. "The Problem Behavior Questionnaire: A Teacher-Based Instrument to Develop Functional Hypotheses of Problem Behavior in General Education Classrooms." *Diagnostique* 19, 2–3 (1994), pp. 103–115.

Lewis-Palmer, Teri, George Sugai, and S. Larson. "Using Data to Guide Decisions About Program Implementation and Effectiveness." *Effective School Practices* 17, 4 (1999), pp. 47–53.

Lipsey, Mark W., and David B. Wilson. "The Efficacy of Psychological, Educational, and Behavioral Treatment: Confirmation from Meta-analysis." *American Psychologist* 48, 12 (1993), pp. 1181–1209.

Martella, Ronald C., and J. Ron Nelson. "Managing Classroom Behaviour." *Journal of Direct Instruction* 3 (2003), pp. 139–165.

Marzano, Robert J., Jana S. Marzano, and Debra J. Pickering. *Classroom Management That Works: Research-Based Strategies for Every Teacher.* Alexandria, VA: Association for Supervision and Curriculum Development, 2003.

Musselwhite, Caroline Ramsey, and Linda J. Burkhart. "Can We Chat? Co-planned Sequenced Social Scripts: A Make It / Take It Book of Ideas and Adaptations" (booklet). Litchfield Park, AZ: Special Communications, 2001.

Neel, Richard S., K. Kay Cessna, Jaclyn Borock, and Sue Bechard. "Quality Program Indicators for Children with Emotional and Behavior Disorders." *Beyond Behavior,* Spring (2003), pp. 3–9.

Nelson, J. Ron, Ronald M. Martella, and Nancy Marchand-Martella. "Maximizing Student Learning: The Effects of a Comprehensive School-Based Program for Preventing Problem Behaviors." *Journal of Emotional and Behavioral Disorders* 10, 3 (2002), pp. 136–148.

Porter, Gordon L., et al. "Problem Solving Teams: A Thirty-Minute Peer-Helping Model." In Gordon L. Porter and Diane Richler (eds.), *Changing Canadian Schools: Perspectives on Disability and Inclusion* (North York, ON: The Roeher Institute, 1991), pp. 224–228.

Richardson, Brent G., and Margery J. Shupe. "The Importance of Teacher Self-Awareness in Working with Students with Emotional and Behavioral Disorders." *Teaching Exceptional Children* 36, 2 (November/December 2003), pp. 8–13.

Scott, Terrance M., and Deborah B. Caron. "Conceptualizing Functional Behavior Assessment as Prevention Practice Within Positive Behavior Support Systems." *Preventing School Failure* 50, 1 (Fall 2005), pp. 13–20.

Scott, Terrance M., and Judi Hunter. "Initiating Schoolwide Support Systems: An Administrator's Guide to the Process." *Beyond Behavior* 11, 1 (2001), pp. 13–15.

Scott, Terrance M., Carl J. Liaupsin, C. Michael Nelson, and Kristine Jolivette. "Ensuring Student Success Through Team-Based Functional Behavioral Assessment." *Teaching Exceptional Children* 35, 5 (May/June 2003), pp. 16–21.

Scott, Terrance M., and C. Michael Nelson. "Using Functional Behavioral Assessment to Develop Effective Intervention Plans: Practical Classroom Applications." *Journal of Positive Behavior Interventions* 1, 4 (Fall 1999), pp. 242–251.

Scott, Terrance M., C. Michael Nelson, and Joy Zabala. "Functional Behavior Assessment Training in Public Schools: Facilitating Systemic Change." *Journal of Positive Behavior Interventions* 5, 4 (Fall 2003), pp. 216–224.

Seip, Jo-Anne. *Teaching Students with Autism and Developmental Delays: A Guide for Staff Training and Development.* Delta, BC: Gateway Press, 1996.

Souveny, Dwaine M., and Dianna L. Souveny. *The ABCs for Success: Attention Deficit Disorders.* Revised ed. Red Deer, AB: Dynamic Networks, 2000.

Sprague, Jeff, and Annemieke Golly. *Best Behavior: Building Positive Behavior Support in Schools.* Longmont, CO: Sopris West Educational Services, 2005.

Sprick, Randall S. *Discipline in the Secondary Classroom: A Positive Approach to Behavior Management.* 2nd ed. San Francisco, CA: John Wiley & Sons, Inc., 2006.

Sprick, Randall, Marilyn Sprick, and Mickey Garrison. *Foundations: Developing Positive School-wide Discipline Policies.* Longmont, CO: Sopris West, 1992.

Sugai, George, and Robert H. Horner. "The Evolution of Discipline Practices: School-wide Positive Behavior Supports." *Child and Family Behavior Therapy* 24, 1/2 (2002), pp. 23–50.

Sugai, George, et al. "Applying Positive Behavioral Support and Functional Behavioral Assessment in Schools." *Journal of Positive Behavioral Interventions* 2, 3 (2000), pp. 131–143.

Sulzer-Azaroff, Beth, and G. Roy Mayer. *Achieving Educational Excellence: Behavior Analysis for Achieving Classroom and Schoolwide Behavior Change.* San Marcos, CA: Western Image, 1994.

Talbot, Laura A., and D. Barry Lumden. "On the Association Between Humor and Burnout." *Humor: International Journal of Humor Research* 13, 4 (2000), pp. 419–428.

Wilde, Jerry. *Hot Stuff to Help Kids Chill Out: The Anger Management Book.* East Troy, WI: LGR Publishing, 1997.

# Index